NFT MASTERCLASS

Exploring the Digital Future in Art,
Investments, and Creativity.

Lex Digitalis

Independently published

Cod ISBN: 9798878648974

Cover design by: Art Painter
Library of Congress Control Number: 2018675309
Printed in the United States of America

To those who delve into these pages filled with knowledge and innovation, we dedicate this journey into the universe of Non-Fungible Tokens (NFTs). This guide is crafted for you, adventurers of the new digital era, explorers of financial frontiers, and creatives seeking new horizons.

To you, brave readers, embarking on this path to understand the revolutionary potential of NFTs, we dedicate these words. Whether you are newcomers to blockchain technology or industry veterans, we hope this guide provides a clear perspective, inspiration, and a map to navigate the vast world of NFTs.

To the visionaries who dare to imagine a future where digital ownership is decentralized and authenticated by the blockchain, we invite you to dream with us. These pages celebrate your curiosity and thirst for knowledge, a light illuminating the path through the intricate tapestries of NFTs.

To those seeking new ways to create, sell, and purchase digital art, to those wishing to leverage the financial opportunities of NFTs, to those dreaming of owning a unique piece of this digital future, we welcome you. This guide is an invitation to explore, learn, and, above all, dream big.

Whether you are here to gain practical skills in buying and selling NFTs or to deeply understand the technology that fuels them, rest assured that this journey is designed for you. We will accompany you through the depths of the blockchain, explore inspiring success stories, and guide you in recognizing the opportunities the world of NFTs offers.

These pages are dedicated to you, pioneers of the new digital frontier, where art, finance, and technology converge to create a unique and extraordinary landscape. May this journey enrich you with knowledge, inspiration, and, above all, provide you with the keys to unlock the doors of a digital future that only NFTs can offer.

Welcome to this journey, and may your minds be open to the infinite possibilities of Non-Fungible Tokens.

"Lex Digitalis is the symphony of the digital future, the score that guides the dance of algorithms on the vast stage of the blockchain. In this technological ballet, digital law directs the choreography, outlining the spaces where trust, transparency, and authenticity blend into a harmonious step towards a new digital paradigm."

LEX DIGITALIS

CONTENTS

INTRODUCTION

In the ever-changing fabric of the digital revolution, where innovation is the constant and technology serves as a catalyst for change, we find ourselves facing a phenomenon that challenges the very foundations of our concept of digital ownership and transactions: Non-Fungible Tokens (NFTs). This book, "Lex Digitalis: Comprehensive Guide to NFTs," is an in-depth perspective on this revolutionary technology, conceived as a guiding light for those who wish to explore, understand, and capitalize on the unprecedented potential of NFTs.

The Frontier of Digital Ownership:

Imagine a world where the concept of ownership is no longer limited to the physical but extends to a universe of unique digital assets, represented by Non-Fungible Tokens. This is the frontier of digital ownership, an unexplored territory where every element, from artistic creativity to virtual identity, can be authenticated, owned, and exchanged on the blockchain.

Blockchain as the Foundation:

To fully grasp NFTs, we must traverse the paths of blockchain, the revolutionary technology at the core of this innovation. We will examine blockchain in all its aspects, from an immutable and decentralized data structure to a mechanism that has the power to rewrite the rules of digital interaction. The blockchain is the stage on which NFTs perform, creating a secure and authenticated digital ecosystem.

The Promise of NFTs:

NFTs come with a bold promise: to transform the perception of digital value. From digital artworks to unique pieces of virtual content, NFTs offer authenticity and rarity, changing the way we perceive and attribute value to digital assets. In this book, we will explore how this digital revolution is redefining the very concept of ownership.

The Race of Digital "New Rich":

In the last two years, the phenomenon of digital "new rich" has emerged as a side effect of the NFT rush. Individuals with significant financial resources have seen in NFTs a unique opportunity to expand their wealth. We will analyze the reasons behind this influx, narrating success stories that attest to the financial potential of this innovative technology.

Generating Extra Income with NFTs:

If you are looking for ways to generate extra income, NFTs might be the key to unlocking new opportunities. We will explore how to start earning in a simple and secure way with Non-Fungible Tokens, providing practical advice for those looking to capitalize on this rapidly growing phenomenon.

The Depth of NFTs:

A chapter entirely dedicated to an in-depth understanding of NFTs will take us to the heart of this technology, unveiling the meaning behind those four letters and explaining how blockchain technology is redefining the very concept of digital tokenization. A thorough knowledge of this technology is crucial to fully harness its potential.

Success Stories and Creation of Personal NFTs:

We will recount success stories of those who have successfully navigated the waters of NFTs, generating significant profits through unique strategies. For those who wish to be actively involved, we will also explore the process of creating, buying, and selling personal NFTs, providing practical tips to maximize profits.

Promotion Strategies and Best Platforms:

Once you have created your NFT, success depends on the ability to promote it effectively. We will explore safe and successful promotion strategies, along with a detailed guide to the best platforms and websites for informed and secure investment in the world of NFTs.

Risk Management and Future Projects:

Every investment involves risks, and NFTs are no exception. We will delve into intelligent risk management, providing advice on how to protect your capital while exploring the opportunities offered by this technology. Additionally, we will analyze high-potential NFT projects, helping you identify the future stars of the market.

Passive Income Opportunity and the Explosion of Collections:

NFTs are not just a source of instant gain but can also generate passive income over time. We will explore how to capitalize on this opportunity, growing your wealth without having to dedicate many hours a day. Knowing the right information and collections ready to explode in the market is crucial to take advantage of the rise of NFTs.

Preparing for the Future of NFTs:

The world of NFTs is constantly evolving, and preparing for the future means understanding emerging trends and always staying one step ahead in the rapidly changing market. We will explore how to do this and how to keep up with an industry that develops at a dizzying pace.

Essential Tools and NFTs in the World of Digital Art:

Being a successful NFT investor requires using the right tools. We will introduce you to the essential tools needed to monitor, manage, and optimize your NFT portfolio. We will also explore the combination of NFTs and digital art, analyzing how this technology has revolutionized the way artists can monetize their talent.

Crypto Art, CryptoPunks, and NFTs in the Gaming World:

The book will also delve into the world of Crypto Art, examining its explosive growth and its impact on the NFT market. We will dedicate a thorough look at CryptoPunks, becoming true symbols in the world of NFTs, analyzing their history and iconic status. We will also explore how NFTs are revolutionizing the gaming industry, influencing how players own and exchange virtual assets in games.

Tokenization of Real Assets and NFTs in the Music Industry:

One of the most intriguing applications of NFTs is the tokenization of real assets, such as real estate and land. We will analyze how this practice is changing the way we own and invest in physical property. We will also explore how musical artists are increasingly embracing NFTs, using them to distribute their music, engage with fans, and create new sources of income.

Regulation, Sustainability, and Investor Psychology:

With the rapid growth of the NFT market, the issue of regulation has become increasingly relevant. We will discuss current and future laws that could influence the world of NFTs and investors. We will also address the crucial aspect of environmental sustainability, exploring how Blockchain technology and NFTs can coexist sustainably. We will examine how investor psychology plays a role in the NFT market, influencing decisions and investment trends.

The Importance of Community and Advanced Resources:

Communities play a crucial role in the success of NFTs. We will analyze how community dynamics influence the value and longevity of an NFT project and how you can actively participate in these communities. For those who want to further deepen their understanding and expertise in the world of NFTs, we will provide a list of advanced resources, from online forums to analytical tools, to stay updated and informed.

Frequently Asked Questions, Conclusions, and Future Perspectives:

We will answer the most common questions that investors and enthusiasts have about NFTs, providing clarity on complex concepts and practical aspects of this innovative technology. We will conclude this guide with a reflection on the potential of NFTs and future prospects, exploring how this technology will continue to evolve and influence the way we live, invest, and perceive digital value.

Welcome to "Lex Digitalis: Comprehensive Guide to NFTs." We are ready to embark on this journey together, exploring the endless opportunities that NFTs offer in the constantly evolving digital landscape.

PREFACE

In the vast landscape of digital innovation, where technology evolves at an unprecedented pace, we find ourselves facing a revolution that has captured the imagination and ambitions of individuals from every corner of the globe: Non-Fungible Tokens (NFTs).

This book, dedicated to anyone fascinated by the digital future, is an invitation to explore the intricate paths of blockchain, to understand the potential of NFTs, and to embrace a world where digital ownership is uniquely and securely authenticated.

A Journey into Blockchain:

The beginning of this journey takes us to the heart of blockchain, that revolutionary technology that gave life to NFTs. We will explore the foundations of blockchain, an immutable and decentralized data structure that has the power to redefine the very concept of trust and authenticity in the digital world.

NFTs: A World of Opportunities:

NFTs emerge as protagonists in this narrative, introducing us to a world where each token represents a unique and inimitable piece of digital value. Throughout the pages of this book, we will discover how NFTs have catalyzed the creation, sale, and purchase of digital art, transforming the enjoyment of art into an experience authenticated by the blockchain.

The Rise of Digital "New Rich":

In the chapter dedicated to NFT investments, we take a look at the phenomenon of digital "new rich," those who have embarked on the path of NFTs and have exponentially grown their wealth. We will explore the reasons behind this investment frenzy, analyzing success stories that serve as inspiration for those aspiring to navigate the waters of NFTs.

Generating Income with Non-Fungible Tokens:

If you are looking for a way to generate extra income, the chapter dedicated to income generation with NFTs is your travel companion. We will explore ways to earn safely and simply, leveraging the opportunity offered by Non-Fungible Tokens.

The Depth of NFTs:

We will embark on a journey into the depths of NFTs, revealing what lies behind those letters and how this phenomenon has generated millions of dollars for those who have recognized its potential. Understanding the technology behind NFTs is the first step to fully capitalize on their value.

Success Stories and Creation of Personal NFTs:

We will discover the stories of those who have capitalized on this innovation, generating millions of dollars through NFTs. Moreover, for those who wish to actively enter the world of NFTs, the chapter dedicated to creating personal NFTs will be a practical guide on how to create, buy, and sell your own Non-Fungible Tokens to maximize profits.

Safe Promotion and Best Websites for Investment:

Once you have created your NFT, success will depend on your ability to promote it effectively. We will explore safe and successful promotion strategies, as well as the best websites and platforms for informed investment in the NFT market.

Risk Management and Future Projects:

We will also address the crucial issue of risk management in NFT investments, providing advice on how to protect your capital in this dynamic world. We will also analyze high-potential NFT projects, guiding you in choosing the next market trends.

Passive Income Opportunity and the Explosion of Collections:

NFTs are not just a source of instant gain but can also generate passive income over time. We will explore how to capitalize on this opportunity, growing your wealth without having to dedicate many hours a day. Moreover, to take advantage of the rise of NFTs, it is crucial to know the right information and the collections that are about to explode in the market.

Preparing for the Future of NFTs:

The world of NFTs is constantly evolving, and preparing for the future means understanding emerging trends and always staying one step ahead in the rapidly changing market. We will explore how to do this and how to keep up with an industry that develops at a dizzying pace.

Essential Tools and NFTs in the World of Digital Art:

Being a successful NFT investor requires using the right tools. We will introduce you to the essential tools needed to monitor, manage, and optimize your NFT portfolio. We will also explore the combination of NFTs and digital art, analyzing how this technology has revolutionized the way artists can monetize their talent.

Crypto Art, CryptoPunks, and NFTs in the Gaming World:

The book will also delve into the world of Crypto Art, examining its explosive growth and how artists and collectors embrace this form of digital artistic expression. We will dedicate an entire chapter to CryptoPunks, true icons in the world of NFTs, examining their history, impact, and how they have become status symbols in the Non-Fungible Token market. We will also explore the role of NFTs in the gaming industry, discussing how they are revolutionizing the way players own and exchange virtual assets within games.

Tokenization of Real Assets, NFTs in Music, and Regulation:

One of the most intriguing applications of NFTs is the tokenization of real assets, such as real estate and land. We will explore how this practice is changing the way we own and invest in physical property. We will also analyze how musicians are embracing NFTs to distribute their music, engage with fans, and create new sources of income. Furthermore, we will address the growing relevance of laws and regulations in the realm of NFTs.

Environmental Sustainability, Communities, and Investor Psychology:

In an era where environmental sustainability is a critical consideration, we will explore how Blockchain technology and NFTs can coexist sustainably, addressing environmental concerns. We will analyze the importance of communities in the success of NFTs, discussing how community dynamics influence the value and longevity of an NFT project.

Additionally, we will examine how investor psychology plays a role in the NFT market, influencing decisions and investment trends.

Advanced Resources, Frequently Asked Questions, and Conclusions:

We conclude this guide by providing a list of advanced resources, from online forums to analytical tools, for those who wish to deepen their understanding and expertise in the world of NFTs. We will answer the most common questions that investors and enthusiasts have about NFTs, providing clarity on complex concepts and practical aspects of this innovative technology. We will conclude with a reflection on the potential of NFTs and future prospects, exploring how this technology will continue to evolve and influence the way we live, invest, and perceive digital value.

In this journey through the pages of "Lex Digitalis: Comprehensive Guide to NFTs," we hope that every reader finds inspiration, knowledge, and practical tools to explore the vast universe of Non-Fungible Tokens. Welcome to this digital future, where blockchain and NFTs open doors to new possibilities, challenges, and opportunities.

PROLOGUE

In an era characterized by the fusion of the real and digital worlds, Blockchain technology and Non-Fungible Tokens (NFTs) emerge as pioneers of a revolution that will change our conception of ownership, art, and value. This prologue is our invitation to immerse yourself in a journey through the digital future, an exploration that will lead you through the intricate paths of blockchain and NFTs, revealing a universe of unprecedented opportunities.

The World of NFTs: A Universe of Possibilities:

You will enter a world where the distinction between the tangible and intangible blurs, where the very concept of ownership takes on a new form. NFTs, powered by blockchain technology, have opened the doors to an unexplored universe of possibilities. Imagine owning a unique digital artwork, a token that authentically represents the artist's creativity. Moreover, imagine that this token, thanks to the blockchain, cannot be duplicated or counterfeited, giving it authentic and intrinsic value.

The Blockchain Revolution:

To fully understand NFTs, we must start with the blockchain, the technological foundation that has made this digital revolution possible. The blockchain is much more than a simple chain of blocks; it is a decentralized network of nodes working together to create an immutable and secure ledger. Through this technology, NFTs gain their authenticity and trace, eliminating the risk of counterfeiting and providing a new paradigm for transparency and digital integrity.

Digital "New Rich" and the NFT Rush:

In the last two years, we have witnessed the emergence of a new class of digital "new rich," individuals who have seized the opportunity to invest in NFTs. But what drove them to this digital race? This prologue takes a look at the reasons behind the influx of those who see NFTs as a way to increase their wealth. Through success stories, you will discover how some have transformed NFT investments into significant profits.

Generating Income with NFTs: A Practical Approach:

If you've ever wondered how to start earning with NFTs, this book offers a practical and secure approach. Explore strategies and tactics to generate extra income through Non-Fungible Tokens, gaining a detailed understanding of how to enter this ever-expanding world.

What Is an NFT and How Does It Work: A Deep Dive:

Immerse yourself in the detailed explanation of what NFTs really are and how they work. We will delve into the process of creating, exchanging, and owning these unique tokens, revealing the details that make this technology so revolutionary.

Success Stories: An Island of Inspiration:

This prologue presents you with some success stories, testimonials from individuals who have successfully navigated the NFT landscape, generating extraordinary profits. These are stories that inspire and demonstrate the financial and creative potential of this innovative technology.

Creating Your Own NFT: An Act of Authenticity and Creativity:

If your interest is to actively engage in the world of NFTs, we will explore the process of creating your NFT. This is not only an act of authenticity but also of creative expression and innovation.

Promotion Strategies and Best Platforms: The Art of Making Your NFT Shine:

Once you own your NFT, the next challenge is to make it shine in the vast digital world. Explore safe and successful promotion strategies, along with a detailed guide to the best platforms and websites for informed and secure investment in the world of NFTs.

Managing Risks in NFT Investments: A Prudent Approach:

Every investment comes with risks, and NFTs are no exception. In this prologue, we will examine how to manage risks intelligently, protecting your capital while exploring the opportunities offered by this technology.

High-Potential NFT Projects: Navigating the Waters of Innovation:

Navigating the vast world of NFTs requires accurate guidance. We will analyze NFT projects that show high potential for growth and success in the future, helping you identify the future stars of the market.

Passive Income Opportunity with NFTs: Investing Over Time:

NFTs are not just a source of instant gain but can also generate passive income over time. This prologue explores how to capitalize on this opportunity, growing your wealth without having to dedicate many hours a day.

The Explosion of NFT Collections: Identifying Hidden Opportunities:

To take advantage of the rise of NFTs, it is crucial to know the right information and collections that are about to explode in the market. This prologue will be your guide to identifying hidden opportunities and capitalizing on them.

Preparing for the Future of NFTs: Constant Adaptation:

The world of NFTs is constantly evolving. We will explore emerging trends and discuss how to prepare for the future of NFTs, ensuring that you always stay one step ahead in the rapidly changing market.

Essential Tools for NFT Investors: The Key to Success:

As a successful NFT investor, it is crucial to have the right tools. This prologue will introduce you to the essential tools needed to monitor, manage, and optimize your NFT portfolio, ensuring a safe guide through digital waters.

NFTs in the World of Digital Art: An Artistic Exploration:

We will explore the combination of NFTs and digital art, analyzing how this technology has revolutionized the way artists can monetize their talent and how collectors can own unique digital artworks.

Crypto Art and Its Explosive Growth: The Charm of Digital Expression:

The chapter will focus on the expansion of the Crypto Art world, examining how artists and collectors are embracing this form of digital artistic expression and the financial opportunities associated with it.

CryptoPunks - Icons of the NFT World: History and Status:

CryptoPunks have become true icons in the world of NFTs. We will examine their history, impact, and how they have become status symbols in the Non-Fungible Token market.

NFTs in the Gaming World: The Ludic Revolution:

NFTs are also revolutionizing the gaming industry. We will discuss how Non-Fungible Tokens are influencing how players own and exchange virtual goods within games.

Tokenization of Real Assets through NFTs: Beyond the Digital:

One of the most intriguing applications of NFTs is the tokenization of real assets, such as real estate and land. We will explore how this practice is changing the way we own and invest in physical property.

NFTs in the Music Industry: Digital Harmony:

The world of music is increasingly embracing NFTs. We will examine how artists can use Non-Fungible Tokens to distribute their music, engage with fans, and create new sources of income.

Regulation and Laws on NFTs: A Necessary Balance:

With the rapid growth of the NFT market, the issue of regulation has become increasingly relevant. We will discuss current and future laws that could influence the world of NFTs and investors.

NFTs and Environmental Sustainability: A Global Commitment:

Environmental considerations have become critical in the NFT industry. We will explore how Blockchain technology and NFTs can coexist sustainably, addressing environmental concerns.

The Importance of the NFT Community: A Solid Foundation:

Communities play a crucial role in the success of NFTs. We will analyze how community dynamics influence the value and longevity of an NFT project and how you can actively participate in these communities.

Investor Psychology in NFTs: A Journey into the Mind:

Investments are often influenced by human psychology. We will examine how investor psychology plays a role in the NFT market, influencing decisions and investment trends.

Advanced Resources for NFT Investors: Discovering Innovation:

For those who want to further deepen their understanding and expertise in the world of NFTs, we will provide a list of advanced resources, from online forums to analytical tools, to stay updated and informed.

Frequently Asked Questions about NFTs: Clear Answers for Digital Clarity:

We will answer the most common questions that investors and enthusiasts have about NFTs, providing clarity on complex concepts and practical aspects of this innovative technology.

Conclusions and Future Perspectives: A Greeting to the New

Digital:

We will conclude this guide with a reflection on the potential of NFTs and future prospects. We will explore how this technology will continue to evolve and influence the way we live, invest, and perceive digital value.

Welcome aboard "Lex Digitalis: Comprehensive Guide to NFTs." We are ready to guide you through the digital depths of NFTs, illuminating the path to a digital future rich in opportunities and innovation.

CHAPTER 1: INTRODUCTION TO NFTS

In the contemporary digital landscape, Non-Fungible Tokens (NFTs) are emerging as a revolutionary force, radically transforming our understanding of ownership and the transaction of digital assets. This innovation, powered by blockchain technology, is destined to shape the financial destiny of millions of individuals, opening new doors in the worlds of finance and creative expression.

NFTs: Definition

and Meaning The

Digital Property

Revolution

Let's embark on our journey into the world of NFTs by tackling the fundamental concept of digital property. NFTs represent unique and indivisible assets, allowing users to exclusively own digital goods such as artworks, collectibles, games, and much more. Unlike traditional cryptocurrencies like Bitcoin and Ethereum, NFTs bring with them a distinctive element: irreversibility.

The Basic Technology: Blockchain

Blockchain, the driving force behind NFTs, deserves an in-depth analysis. It is a decentralized chain of blocks, where each block contains cryptographic information linked to the previous block. This structure provides transparency, immutability, and security, ensuring that NFTs are authentic and unalterable. Blockchain creates a distributed public ledger, eliminating the need for intermediaries and enabling secure and verifiable transactions.

The Financial Impact of NFTs

The Explosive Growth of the Market

In recent years, the NFT market has experienced explosive growth, attracting the attention of investors, collectors, and artists. The opportunity to monetize digital assets has created a new class of wealth, with a growing number of individuals seeing NFTs as an unprecedented earning opportunity. This influx of "new wealth" is a tangible sign of the transformation underway in the global financial landscape.

Speed and Earning Potential

What sets NFTs apart is the speed with which they can generate significant profits. Thanks to the ease with which they can be created, traded, and owned, NFTs offer a quick and efficient way to capitalize on digital works, games, and other virtual content. This potential for instant earnings has captured the attention of those seeking agile and innovative financial opportunities.

Exploring the Mystery of NFTs

The Need to Understand Blockchain

For many, the underlying technology of NFTs, Blockchain, remains a mystery. This chapter aims to dispel that mystery, providing a clear understanding of how Blockchain works and how its application in NFTs is changing the financial and creative landscape.

A Detailed Analysis of NFTs

We further delve into the meaning of NFTs, examining how these tokens are created, traded, and owned. Through a detailed perspective, we discover how NFTs are revolutionizing the very concept of digital ownership and how they can be leveraged to generate income in innovative ways.

Conclusion

In this introductory chapter, we have laid the foundation for a comprehensive understanding of the world of NFTs. We explored the meaning behind the concept of digital property, analyzed the Blockchain technology that makes it possible, and assessed the financial impact of NFTs in contemporary society. In the continuation of the guide, we will delve deeper into each of these aspects, providing a complete framework that will enable readers to acquire a solid knowledge and fully capitalize on the opportunities offered by NFTs.

CHAPTER 2: DEMYSTIFYING BLOCKCHAIN

To embark on a comprehensive journey into the world of NFTs, it is essential to take an in-depth look at the foundations that support them: Blockchain. In this chapter, we will demystify this emerging technology, exploring how Blockchain has the potential to revolutionize society and the management of digital assets, opening unimaginable scenarios until not long ago.

The Birth of

Blockchain

Origins and

Evolution

To fully understand Blockchain, we must trace its roots. It originated as an integral part of Bitcoin, the first cryptocurrency, developed in 2008 by an individual or group of people using the pseudonym Satoshi Nakamoto. Blockchain was conceived as a distributed ledger to securely and transparently track Bitcoin transactions. Since then, it has evolved and expanded its scope, becoming a key technology for NFTs and much more.

Blockchain Architecture

Blocks and Chains: The Basic Structure

The heart of Blockchain is its block structure, each containing a set of verified transactions. Blocks are cryptographically linked, creating an immutable chain of information. We will examine in detail how this system ensures data security and integrity, eliminating the risk of manipulation or fraud.

Fundamental Principles of

Blockchain Decentralization

and Consensus

Demystifying Blockchain requires understanding fundamental principles such as decentralization and consensus. Decentralization means that the management and recording of transactions are not concentrated in a single entity but distributed among many nodes in the network. Consensus, on the other hand, implies that transactions must be approved by the majority of network participants before being added to a block. These concepts are crucial to ensuring a secure and tamper resistant Blockchain.

Types of Blockchain

Public, Private, and Consortium

There are different types of Blockchain, each with specific characteristics. Public Blockchains are accessible to anyone and transparent, as in the case of Bitcoin and Ethereum. Private Blockchains, in contrast, are limited to a closed group of users, often used in business environments. Consortium Blockchains are a hybrid, where multiple entities manage the network by sharing responsibilities.

We will explore how these variations can affect the security

and accessibility of Blockchains. Smart Contracts

Automating Transactions

A fundamental element of Blockchain is the ability to implement smart contracts. These are self- executing contracts that automate the execution of programmable agreements without the need for intermediaries. We will see how smart contracts are revolutionizing the way transactions are handled, ensuring the execution of predetermined conditions transparently and without ambiguity.

Applications Beyond

Cryptocurrencies Beyond

Bitcoin and Ethereum

While Bitcoin introduced the concept of Blockchain, many other cryptocurrencies, such as Ethereum, have brought key innovations. Beyond cryptocurrencies, Blockchain finds applications in sectors such as food traceability, supply chain management, and even digital elections. We will analyze how Blockchain technology is influencing various aspects of our daily lives.

Transformative Potential

Revolution in Digital Asset Management

Blockchain is rapidly becoming a catalyst for transformation in how we manage digital assets. Through transparent, decentralized, and secure management, Blockchain offers an innovative way to conceive and manage digital property. We will discuss how this technology can eliminate intermediaries and foster a fairer and more efficient environment for users.

Challenges

and Criticisms

Scalability and

Sustainability

Despite its potential, Blockchain is not immune to challenges. We will critically examine issues related to scalability, as the growing number of transactions could strain network capacity.

Additionally, we will address the issue of environmental

sustainability, as some Blockchains require considerable energy resources.

Conclusion

The chapter on demystifying Blockchain has provided us with a deep understanding of this fundamental technology. We explored its origins, analyzed the architecture, understood key principles such as decentralization and consensus, examined types of Blockchain, and evaluated applications beyond cryptocurrencies. Blockchain is the engine powering NFTs, and armed with this knowledge, we are ready to delve further into the fascinating and innovative world of unique digital transactions.

CHAPTER 3: THE FRENZY OF NFT INVESTMENTS

Over the past two years, an extraordinary phenomenon has shaken the financial world: the frenzy of NFT investments. A considerable number of individuals with significant financial means have seen these Non-Fungible Tokens as a unique opportunity to expand their wealth. In this chapter, we will explore the reasons behind this growing influx of "new wealthy" into the world of NFTs, analyzing market dynamics, unique opportunities, and driving factors of this unprecedented phenomenon.

The NFT Boom: A Tale of

Explosive Growth Defining

the Boom

The frenzy of NFT investments can only be understood in the context of the boom that has characterized this sector. Over the past two years, the NFT market has experienced exponential growth, attracting the attention of artists, collectors, celebrities, and investors worldwide. This boom has contributed to redefining the concept of digital value and has opened new financial opportunities for those able to seize them.

The New Wealth

of NFTs Investor

Profiles

Who are these "new wealthy" individuals who have embraced NFTs? In many cases, they are individuals with a visionary outlook and considerable financial means. They have identified NFTs as a class of digital assets capable of generating significant returns in a relatively short period. Let's explore the profiles and motivations of those who have contributed to making NFTs synonymous with financial prosperity.

Reasons Behind the

Growth Scarcity and

Uniqueness

One of the key factors fueling the frenzy of NFT investments is the scarcity and uniqueness of these tokens. The indivisible and non-replicable nature of NFTs makes them desirable and valuable. This inherent scarcity translates into intrinsic value that has attracted investors seeking unique and irreplicable digital assets.

Creative Expression and Digital Identity

NFTs are not just financial assets; they are also expressions of creativity and digital identity. Artists, musicians, and creatives from various disciplines have embraced NFTs as a new form of expression and monetization. The opportunity to own unique and authentic digital artworks has expanded the investor audience, contributing to market growth.

Transaction Speed and Accessibility

The speed at which NFTs can be created, bought, and sold is another key element. Investors are drawn to the quick entry and exit from the market, capitalizing on price fluctuations. The ease of access, thanks to blockchain technology, has opened the world of NFTs to a wide range of participants, making this sector accessible even to those new to digital investments.

The Rise of Digital
Collectors Collecting
in the Virtual World

The figure of the digital collector has emerged as a key player in the frenzy of NFT investments. The possibility of owning exclusive digital collections, such as CryptoPunks and Bored Ape Yacht Club, has catalyzed the interest of those who see NFTs as a new form of collecting. Explore how collectors are contributing to the growth of the sector, making NFTs an integral part of contemporary digital culture.

The Role of Celebrities and

Brands Endorsements and

Collaborations

The interest of celebrities and brands has significantly contributed to the surge in NFT investments. From digital artworks to virtual fashion collections, collaborations with famous personalities and renowned brands have amplified the visibility of NFTs. Examine how such endorsements have influenced public perception and demand for NFTs.

Instant Earning

Opportunities

Immediate Returns

The possibility of achieving substantial profits in the short term has been one of the main attractions for investors. Some have generated gains of 5-700% in just a few days, leveraging NFT price fluctuations. This element of immediate earning opportunities has created a frenetic dynamic in the market, fueling the influx of new participants.

The Role of

NFT Platforms

Marketplaces and

Virtual Galleries

NFT platforms, such as OpenSea, Rarible, and Foundation, play a crucial role in facilitating exchanges and showcasing digital artworks. Explore how these platforms have contributed to creating an ecosystem where artists can reach a wide audience, and investors can access a broad range of NFTs.

The   Investment   Frenzy:

Sustainability   and   Risks

Environmental   Sustainability

and Financial Risks

Despite extraordinary growth, the frenzy of NFT investments has raised concerns about the environmental sustainability of blockchains and the financial risks associated with a still-developing market. We will critically address these aspects, examining how the sector can balance enthusiasm with long-term responsibility.

Conclusions

The frenzy of NFT investments has redefined how we perceive digital value and investment. Through scarcity, uniqueness, creative expression, and the potential for quick gains, NFTs have attracted a new wave of investors, transforming many into the "new wealthy." However, sustainability and associated risks require careful assessment. As we further explore the world of NFTs, it is crucial to balance enthusiasm with awareness, seizing opportunities without neglecting the challenges presented by this dynamic sector.

CHAPTER 4: GENERATING EXTRA INCOME WITH NON-FUNGIBLE TOKENS (NFTS)

If you are looking for new opportunities to generate extra income and have heard about Non- Fungible Tokens (NFTs), you are in the right place. In this chapter, we will explore in detail how to start earning in a simple and secure way with NFTs. From creating and selling NFTs to investing and promoting, you will learn how to fully leverage the potential of this innovative technology.

The NFT Revolution in

the Digital Economy

Opportunities for Income

Generation

NFTs have introduced a revolution in the digital economy, offering the possibility to generate income in completely new ways. These unique and indivisible tokens allow users to own and trade digital assets with unprecedented ease. Let's explore how this revolution is opening doors to new income models.

Creating and Selling

Your NFTs From

Concept to Creation

The first step to generate income with NFTs is understanding how to create and sell your tokens. We will examine the basics of NFT creation, including the tools and platforms most suitable for this purpose. From choosing the type of content to tokenize to defining royalties, you will learn how to bring your creativity into the world of NFTs.

Marketplace Platforms

Where to sell your NFTs is as important as their creation. We will analyze the most popular marketplace platforms, such as OpenSea, Rarible, and Mintable, examining the features that make them ideal for artists, content creators, and sellers. These platforms facilitate the meeting between creators and those who want to own NFTs, making the selling process more accessible.

Investing in NFTs: Tips

for Safe Gains Identifying

Investment Opportunities

If creating your own NFTs is not for you, there is still a way to generate income: investing in NFTs. We will explore investment strategies, from identifying promising opportunities to assessing growth potential. You will learn to navigate the vast world of NFTs, focusing on valuable projects and potential returns.

Evaluating Longevity and Appreciation

Investing in NFTs requires an accurate assessment of the longevity and potential appreciation of a project. We will discuss how to analyze factors such as the artist's notoriety, the rarity of the artwork, and high-profile collaborations to determine the long-term value and growth of an NFT.

Promoting and Selling Your

NFTs Securely Marketing

Strategies for Artists and

Creators

Promotion is essential to ensure the success of your NFT sales. We will explore effective marketing strategies for artists and content creators, from building an online presence to partnering with influencers. With the right approach, you can increase the visibility of your digital works and maximize their earning potential.

Security and Rights Protection

Security is a key concern when it comes to selling and buying NFTs. We will address best practices to ensure transaction security and copyright protection. With the growing popularity of NFTs, it is crucial to protect your creativity and investments.

Best Platforms

for NFT Investing

Exploring

Investment Options

If you are considering the option of investing in NFTs, it is important to know the best available platforms. We will analyze the key features of platforms such as Foundation, SuperRare, and NBA Top Shot, providing a comprehensive overview of options available for investors seeking new opportunities.

Upcoming High-

Potential Projects Stay

Updated on Market

Trends

The world of NFTs is constantly evolving, with new projects emerging regularly. We will examine some of the upcoming high-potential projects that could become future market stars. Staying informed about these trends will give you an advantage in finding promising investment opportunities.

Passive Income

Opportunities with NFTs

Working Smartly with Your

Assets

NFTs offer not only active income opportunities but also the possibility of generating passive income. We will explore strategies for working smartly with your digital assets, such as renting artworks or participating in income-generating projects. These options allow you to maximize the earning potential of your NFTs without constant commitment.

Conclusion: Fully Harnessing the Potential of NFTs

In conclusion, this chapter provides a comprehensive overview of how to generate extra income with Non-Fungible Tokens. Whether you are an artist, content creator, or investor, NFTs offer multiple avenues to fully leverage their potential. From creating and selling NFTs to evaluating investment opportunities and promoting safely, this chapter equips you with the necessary knowledge to start generating income simply and securely in the exciting world of NFTs.

CHAPTER 5: WHAT IS AN NFT AND HOW DOES IT WORK

To fully harness the potential of Non-Fungible Tokens (NFTs), it is essential to have a thorough understanding of what they are and how they work. In this chapter, we will examine the concept of NFTs, from their creation to exchange and ownership. This detailed information is crucial for those who want to dive into the world of NFTs with awareness and profitability.

Definition of Non-Fungible

Token (NFT) Uniqueness

and Indivisibility

Non-Fungible Tokens (NFTs) represent a category of unique and indivisible digital assets. Unlike traditional cryptocurrencies such as Bitcoin or Ethereum, which are fungible and can be exchanged equivalently, NFTs are distinctive and cannot be divided into smaller units. This characteristic makes them ideal for representing unique digital objects such as artwork, collectibles, and other virtual content.

Blockchain as the Foundation

At the core of the existence of NFTs is blockchain technology. Each NFT is securely and immutably recorded on a decentralized blockchain. This ensures transparency, authenticity, and integrity of the digital asset, as the information associated with the NFT is encrypted and linked to previous blocks in the chain.

NFT Creation

Process

Tokenization of

Digital Content

The creation of an NFT begins with the process of tokenizing digital content. This content can be anything from a digital artwork to a video, a musical piece, or even a tweet. The creator decides to convert this content into an NFT, giving it a unique and irreplicable value.

NFT Standards: ERC-721 and Others

NFTs follow certain technical standards to ensure their interoperability across different platforms and digital wallets. ERC-721 is one of the most used protocols for creating NFTs on blockchains like Ethereum. There are also other standards, such as ERC-1155, which allows the creation of multiple tokens in a single smart contract.

NFT Market

and Exchange

Marketplace

Platforms

Once created, the NFT can be listed for sale on various specialized marketplace platforms for NFTs. Examples of these platforms include OpenSea, Rarible, and Mintable, offering artists and content creators the opportunity to reach a wide audience of interested buyers.

Purchase and Transfer Process

Buyers can acquire NFTs using cryptocurrencies such as Ethereum. Once the purchase is made, the NFT is transferred to the buyer's digital wallet, making them the new registered owner on the blockchain. This process occurs quickly and securely, thanks to the decentralized nature and blockchain technology.

Ownership and Authenticity of NFTs

Storage in the Digital Wallet

Possessing an NFT is closely tied to the user's digital wallet. A digital wallet is an application or online service that allows users to manage and store their NFTs. Each NFT in the wallet is associated with a private cryptographic key that ensures access and security of digital resources.

Certification of Authenticity

Blockchain technology provides an invaluable certification of authenticity for NFTs. Every transaction and ownership are immutably recorded on the blockchain, creating a chain of custody that documents the complete history of the NFT. This makes NFTs transparent, verifiable, and authentic, essential elements of value for artists and buyers.

Interoperability and

Standardization Portability

Across Different Platforms

Thanks to NFT standards like ERC-721, these tokens can be moved and viewed on various platforms and digital wallets. This interoperability is crucial to ensure that users can fully enjoy their NFTs regardless of the platform used to acquire them.

The Future of NFTs

New Applications and Technological Developments

The world of NFTs is constantly evolving, with new applications and technological developments emerging regularly. Projects such as virtual metaverses, decentralized games, and other innovative uses of NFTs are constantly redefining the landscape. We will examine some emerging trends that could shape the future of NFTs.

Security and Risks

Associated with NFTs

Security Awareness

Security is a key concern when it comes to NFTs. Users must be aware of associated risks, such as fraud or scams, and adopt security practices such as using secure digital wallets and paying attention to reliable marketplace platforms.

Blockchain Scalability

With the increasing popularity of NFTs, the issue of scalability of underlying blockchains has emerged as a challenge. We will discuss proposed solutions and challenges related to managing a growing number of transactions.

Conclusion: Knowledge for Exploitation

Fully understanding what an NFT is and how it works is essential for those who want to fully exploit the potential of this innovative technology. From creation to exchange and ownership, NFTs offer a revolutionary way to conceive and manage digital assets. With the solid foundation provided by this chapter, you are ready to explore the vast and fascinating world of NFTs with informed awareness.

CHAPTER 6: SUCCESS STORIES WITH NFTS

In the vast universe of NFTs, some success stories stand out like beacons, illuminating the path for those seeking to navigate this fascinating world. In this chapter, we will explore some of these stories, revealing how individuals have generated millions of dollars through NFTs. These success tales not only inspire but also demonstrate the revolutionary financial potential of this innovative technology.

CryptoPunks: Pioneers

of NFT Exploration The

CryptoPunks Boom

The year 2017 witnessed the birth of CryptoPunks, a collection of 10,000 uniquely generated 8-bit characters on the Ethereum Blockchain. Initially distributed for free, these characters soon became coveted items within the NFT community. Some fortunate CryptoPunks owners, thanks to the growing popularity of the collection, sold their tokens for millions of dollars. This pioneering story demonstrates how vision and taking initial risks can lead to extraordinary rewards.

Beeple: The

Successful NFT Artist

A Revolution in

Digital Art

The name Beeple (Mike Winkelmann) has become synonymous with success in the realm of NFTs. In March 2021, Beeple sold a digital artwork titled "Everydays: The First 5000 Days" at a Christie's auction for the extraordinary sum of $69 million. This sale propelled Beeple into the realm of digital artists, proving that digital art can be as, if not more, valuable than traditional art. Beeple's story illustrates the revolutionary potential of NFTs in the artistic sector.

NBA Top Shot: Digital Collectibles

in the Sports World The Fusion of

Sports and NFTs

NBA Top Shot introduced NFTs to the world of sports, creating a platform for the digital collection of NBA highlights called "Moments." Users can own and trade these Moments, authenticated by the Blockchain. Some of them have reached notable values, with success stories of sports enthusiasts generating significant profits through the buying and selling of rare and sought-after Moments. This fusion of sports and NFTs has opened new frontiers in the digital collectibles sector.

Bored Ape Yacht Club:

Successful Virtual Collecting A

Digital Collectors' Community

The Bored Ape Yacht Club has become a phenomenon in the world of NFTs, offering anyone owning one of the 10,000 Bored Apes access to an exclusive community and special benefits. Some members have sold their Bored Apes for significant amounts, demonstrating that ownership of an NFT token can extend beyond simple possession, including participation in virtual communities. This story highlights the power of communities in the NFT ecosystem.

Jack Dorsey and the First Tweet:

NFTs for History Tokenizing Historical Moments

Twitter co-founder Jack Dorsey capitalized on the rise of NFTs to tokenize his first tweet. This NFT was sold at auction for over $2.9 million, proving that even digital historical moments can become valuable through this technology. Dorsey's story emphasizes how NFTs can be used to preserve and valorize unique moments in digital history.

Lessons and Insights from

Success Stories Vision,

Creativity, and Calculated

Risks

Success stories with NFTs offer valuable lessons. Vision, creativity, and calculated risks are common elements among many of them. Successful individuals were not afraid to embrace new ideas and experiment. The lessons learned from these stories can be a guiding light for those aspiring to make their mark in the world of NFTs.

Exploring New

Opportunities and Projects

The Ever-Evolving World of

NFTs

With the world of NFTs constantly evolving, new opportunities and projects continue to emerge. Exploring new territories within the sector can be a key to success. Participants who stay informed about the latest trends and innovations can spot new investment and participation opportunities.

Ethical Considerations and

Sustainability Reflecting on

the Ethical Role of NFTs

In the context of success stories with NFTs, it is also important to reflect on the ethical role and sustainability. The growing interest in NFTs has led to increased awareness of issues such as the environmental impact of blockchains and accessibility. Those venturing into the world of NFTs must consider such issues while pursuing success.

Conclusion: Making a Mark in the NFT Ecosystem

Success stories with NFTs are not just narratives of financial prosperity but illuminate the possibilities and potential of this revolutionary technology. Whether they are stories of digital artists, sports enthusiasts, or virtual collectors, these narratives demonstrate that NFTs can open doors to new forms of expression, participation, and income. With inspiration drawn from these stories, anyone entering the world of NFTs can aspire not only to financial success but also to leave a meaningful mark in the ever-evolving ecosystem of NFTs.

CHAPTER 7: CREATING YOUR OWN NFTS FOR PROFIT

If you have the desire to actively enter the world of NFTs and wish to learn strategies for creating, buying, and selling your Non-Fungible Tokens (NFTs) to maximize profits, you are in the right chapter. In this section, we will explore in detail how you can embark on your journey to create and monetize your NFTs, fully leveraging the potential of this revolutionary technology.

Understand Your Vision and

Create Engaging Content Identify

Your Unique Message

Before diving into NFT creation, it's crucial to understand who you are and what message you want to convey through your works. Whether you're an artist, a creative, or an innovator, identifying your unique vision will help you create engaging and distinctive content.

Experiment and Innovate

NFTs offer fertile ground for experimentation and innovation. Don't be afraid to explore new ideas, styles, and concepts. Diversity and originality often attract attention in the NFT community.

Know the Tools and NFT

Creation Platforms Creation

Platforms

Several platforms specialize in NFT creation, each with its own features and functionalities. Some of the most used platforms include Mintable, Rarible, OpenSea, and Foundation. Knowing these platforms will allow you to select the one that best suits your needs and works.

Use Graphic Design Software

To create high-quality NFTs, it's essential to master graphic design programs. Software like Adobe Photoshop, Illustrator, or open-source graphic software like GIMP can be powerful tools for creating digital artworks.

Tokenize Your Content

Using NFT Standards NFT

Standards: ERC-721 and

Others

NFT standards, such as ERC-721 on Ethereum, define the rules and characteristics of each token. Understanding how to use these standards is crucial to ensure that your NFTs are compatible with various platforms and digital wallets.

Mint Your NFTs

The "minting" process involves the actual creation of your NFT. This process may vary depending on the chosen platform but usually involves uploading your content, assigning metadata, and confirming the token's creation.

Determine Pricing and

Royalty Strategy Evaluate

the Value of Your Work

Determining a fair price for your NFTs is a crucial part of the selling process. Evaluate the value of your work considering factors such as your reputation, content originality, and market demand.

Set Royalties

Royalties allow artists to earn a percentage on each resale of their NFT. Deciding the percentage of royalties is a personal choice, but it's essential to strike a balance between encouraging resales and adequately compensating the original creator.

Actively Promote

Your NFTs Build an

Online Presence

A strong online presence is crucial to promote your NFTs. Use social platforms like Twitter, Instagram, and Discord to share your work, connect with the NFT community, and attract potential buyers.

Collaborations and Partnerships

Collaborating with other artists, participating in collaborative projects, or establishing partnerships with influencers can amplify the visibility of your NFTs. Collaboration can lead to new opportunities and connections within the NFT community.

Manage Security and

Rights Protection Digital

Wallet Security

The security of your digital wallet is essential to protect your NFTs and cryptocurrencies. Use secure digital wallets and keep your private key safe.

Licenses and Copyrights

Remember to protect your copyrights and specify licenses associated with your NFTs. This can help you manage the use and distribution of your digital works.

Learn from

Experiences and Adapt

Monitor the Market

and Feedback

The world of NFTs is dynamic and ever evolving. Monitor the market, observe emerging trends, and pay attention to community feedback. Adaptability is crucial to maintaining success over time.

Continue to Experiment and Improve

Never stop seeking new ways to improve and experiment. Success in NFTs is often linked to the ability to innovate and keep your approach fresh.

Participate in NFT

Communities

Connections and

Support

Participating in NFT communities offers connections, support, and opportunities for continuous learning. Discord and forums dedicated to NFTs are excellent places to exchange ideas, get advice, and stay updated on the latest industry news.

Join Virtual Events and Exhibitions

Virtual NFT events and exhibitions provide a unique opportunity to showcase your works and connect with a wider audience. Participating in such events can increase your visibility and credibility within the community.

Conclusion: Maximize the Opportunity of NFTs

Creating your own NFTs for profit is an exciting journey full of possibilities. With a clear vision, strong technical skills, and a well-defined strategy, you can successfully enter the world of NFTs. Remember that innovation, active promotion, and careful management of your digital assets are key to fully leveraging the opportunity of NFTs and maximizing profits in the long term.

CHAPTER 8: PROMOTION STRATEGIES FOR NFTS

Once you've created your precious Non-Fungible Token (NFT), its success depends not only on its intrinsic quality but also on the ability to effectively promote it. In this chapter, we will explore secure and successful promotion strategies to make your NFT shine in the vast digital world of unique and indivisible assets.

Build a Strong

Online Presence

Social Media as an

Ally

Strategic use of social media is crucial for NFT promotion. Leverage platforms like Twitter, Instagram, and Discord to regularly share your works, engage the community, and create anticipation around your upcoming releases. Use relevant hashtags and join ongoing conversations to increase visibility.

Create Engaging Content

In addition to sharing your NFTs, create engaging content that tells the story behind your works. Behind-the-scenes videos, creative processes, and personal anecdotes can emotionally connect the audience to your creations, stimulating interest and participation.

Collaborate with Other

Artists and Collectors

Strength in Collaboration

Collaborating with other artists and collectors can amplify the visibility of your work. Participate in collaborative projects, exchange advice, and provide mutual support. Collaborations can lead to new exposure opportunities and introduce your NFTs to new audiences.

Create Projects with Common Goals

Creating projects with common goals can be an effective way to expand your network. Involve other artists or creatives with similar visions, contributing to building a strong community and mutually promoting your NFTs.

Participate in Virtual Events

and Exhibitions Virtual

Exposure

Participating in NFT virtual events and exhibitions offers a unique opportunity to showcase your works to a wider audience. Many NFT platforms organize online exhibitions and virtual fairs. Take advantage of these opportunities to exhibit your creations, receive reviews, and attract the attention of collectors.

Engage the Audience with Livestreams

Organize livestreams to engage the audience in real-time. During these sessions, you can present your works, answer viewer questions, and offer exclusive previews. The possibility of direct interaction can create a stronger bond between you and your audience.

Use Popular NFT Platforms

Harness the Popularity of OpenSea and Others

Popular NFT platforms like OpenSea, Rarible, and Foundation attract a vast audience of collectors. Publishing your works on these platforms can significantly increase the visibility of your NFTs. Ensure you optimize the information for each NFT, using detailed descriptions and high-quality images.

Participate in Incentive Programs

Some platforms offer incentive programs for artists. Participating in such programs can offer benefits such as reduced fees or special promotions. Keep an eye on these opportunities to maximize the benefits of your presence on a platform.

Launch Targeted Marketing

Campaigns Define Your

Target

For effective promotion, it's essential to define your target audience. Who are the potential buyers of your NFTs? Identifying your audience will help you create more targeted and relevant marketing campaigns.

Email Marketing and Newsletters

Use email marketing to stay in touch with your followers and potential buyers. Send regular newsletters containing previews of new NFTs, behind-the-scenes news, and updates on your artistic activities. Building a list of interested subscribers can be a valuable asset.

Implement Scarcity and

Exclusivity Strategies Limited

Editions and Exclusives

Implementing scarcity and exclusivity strategies can increase the perceived value of your works. Offer limited editions or exclusive pieces to early buyers. This can create a sense of urgency and desirability among potential buyers.

Experiment with Auctions

Online auctions are a popular form of NFT sales. Organize auctions for your most sought-after works, encouraging active buyer participation. Auctions can create a competitive atmosphere that may lead to higher bids.

Create Supportive Content and

Documentaries Document the

Creative Process

Creating supportive content, such as documentaries on the creative process, can offer an in-depth look behind the scenes. These additional contents not only entertain your audience but can also generate more interest in your works.

Podcasts and Interviews

Participate in podcasts or grant interviews on online platforms. These channels provide an opportunity to tell your story, share your experiences in the world of NFTs, and promote your creations to a wider audience.

Monitor and

Adapt Strategies

Data Analysis and

Feedback

Closely monitor performance metrics and gather feedback from the community. Data analysis can provide valuable insights into which strategies are working best. Adapt your promotion tactics based on this data to optimize results.

Maintain Open Communication

Maintain open communication with your audience. Respond to comments, participate in discussions, and demonstrate your commitment to the community. Authentic communication can help build a loyal fan base.

Conclusion: Illuminate Your NFT in the Digital Landscape

Promoting your NFT requires a combination of creativity, strategy, and constant commitment. With a strong online presence, effective collaborations, active participation in events, and targeted communication, you can illuminate your NFT in the vast landscape of unique assets. Continue to experiment, adapt your strategies to market developments, and, above all, enjoy the journey of promoting your one-of-a-kind works.

CHAPTER 9: BEST WEBSITES AND PLATFORMS FOR INVESTING IN NFTS

Navigating the complex world of NFTs requires not only a good dose of creativity but also accurate guidance in choosing the right platforms to invest in a safe and informed manner. In this chapter, we will explore the best websites and platforms that will allow you to dive into the Non-Fungible Token market, helping you make informed and conscious decisions.

OpenSea

The Leading NFT Marketplace

OpenSea is the leading NFT marketplace, known for its vast range of collections and digital artworks. Users can buy, sell, and discover a variety of NFTs, from CryptoPunks to digital artworks by emerging artists. The platform offers an intuitive interface and advanced features, making it an ideal starting point for anyone looking to begin investing in NFTs.

Rarible

Simple Creation and Sale of NFTs

Rarible is a platform that not only allows buying and selling NFTs but also enables artists to create and monetize their works easily. Rarible's distinctive feature is its user-friendly approach for those entering the world of NFT creation. Artists can mint their tokens directly on the platform and list them for sale with just a few clicks.

Foundation

Exclusivity and Curated Selection

Foundation is a platform focused on exclusivity and the curated selection of digital artworks. To participate in Foundation, artists must be invited or go through a selection process. This approach helps ensure a high quality of works on the platform. Buyers can expect a diverse collection of NFTs from talented artists.

Mintable

Simplified Creation and Sale

Mintable is a platform that emphasizes simplifying the process of creating and selling NFTs. Users can easily mint their works, set custom royalty rules, and manage sales directly on the platform. Mintable is suitable for both novice artists and collectors looking to explore the NFT ecosystem.

SuperRare

Curated and Artistic Collections

SuperRare is a platform dedicated to high-quality digital artworks. The platform focuses on curated collections, offering an environment where artists can showcase exclusive works, and collectors can access unique creations. SuperRare has gained popularity for its top-tier artistic selection.

BakerySwap

NFTs in the DeFi World

BakerySwap is a platform that integrates NFTs into the decentralized finance (DeFi) world. In addition to buying and selling NFTs, BakerySwap offers token staking and farming, bringing a DeFi dimension to the NFT ecosystem. For those interested in merging these two rapidly growing spheres, BakerySwap provides an interesting option.

NBA Top Shot

Tokenization of Sports Moments

NBA Top Shot has introduced NFTs to the sports world, allowing fans to own and trade iconic moments from the NBA. With direct involvement in the sports realm, NBA Top Shot is a unique platform that attracts both NFT collectors and basketball enthusiasts.

Sorare

Fantasy Football with NFTs

Sorare combines the world of fantasy football with NFTs. Users can buy, trade, and collect cards of soccer players, which they can then use in fantasy competitions. This platform offers an engaging experience for sports lovers looking to explore NFTs in a different context.

Decentraland

NFTs and the Metaverse

Decentraland is a blockchain-based platform that combines NFTs and the metaverse. Users can buy and own virtual land, create and monetize digital content, and interact with other participants in the virtual world. Decentraland represents a broader vision of NFTs within the context of a growing metaverse.

Axie Infinity

NFTs in the Gaming World

Axie Infinity is a platform that integrates NFTs into the world of blockchain games. Users can own, trade, and play with creatures called Axies. The platform has gained popularity for its innovative approach to combining gaming and NFTs, offering players the opportunity to earn through gameplay.

CryptoKitties

Pioneers of Virtual Collecting

CryptoKitties was one of the first games to introduce the concept of virtual collecting through NFTs. Users can buy, sell, and trade unique digital cats. While surpassed by many other platforms, CryptoKitties played a pioneering role in introducing NFTs to the world of digital collecting.

Binance NFT

NFT Ecosystem on Binance

Binance NFT is part of the Binance ecosystem and provides a dedicated platform for buying, selling, and trading NFTs. The platform supports multiple blockchains, offering a wide range of options for users. Binance NFT benefits from the robust infrastructure of Binance, one of the world's largest cryptocurrency platforms.

WazirX NFT

Exploring NFTs on WazirX

WazirX NFT is part of the WazirX cryptocurrency exchange platform. It offers users the opportunity to explore and purchase a variety of NFTs. Integrated with the exchange platform, WazirX NFT streamlines the process of buying and selling NFTs for WazirX users.

Enjin Marketplace

NFTs on the Enjin Blockchain

Enjin Marketplace is based on the Enjin blockchain and offers a dedicated ecosystem for NFTs linked to the gaming world and gamer communities. The platform supports the creation of NFTs linked to in-game tokens, allowing developers to easily integrate NFTs into their games.

Mintbase

Simplified Creation and Management

Mintbase stands out for simplifying the creation and management of NFTs. Users can easily create their NFTs and even build custom storefronts to showcase their works. Mintbase focuses on empowering artists, allowing them to manage their NFT presence more independently.

Conclusions: Navigating the World of NFTs with Safety and Awareness

Navigating the world of NFTs requires not only a creative mind but also choosing the right platforms for safe investment. Whether you are an artist looking for a platform to showcase your creations or an investor interested in expanding your portfolio with unique digital assets, the diversity of platforms offers opportunities for everyone. Always remember to do your research, stay informed about market trends, and act with awareness as you explore the vast universe of NFTs.

CHAPTER 10: MANAGING RISKS IN NFT INVESTMENTS

Investing in NFTs offers a world of opportunities, but like any form of investment, it's essential to understand and manage associated risks. In this chapter, we will explore in detail how to intelligently address risks related to NFT investments, protecting your capital and maximizing the opportunities offered by this continually evolving technology.

Understanding

Specific NFT Risks

Market Volatility

The NFT market is known for its volatility. The value of an NFT can fluctuate significantly over time, influenced by factors such as market demand, investor interest, and cultural trends. It's crucial to understand that past profits do not guarantee future results, and volatility can be a double-edged sword.

Technological Risks

The blockchain technology underlying NFTs is not immune to technological risks. Cyberattacks, smart contract bugs, and other technical issues can affect the value and security of NFTs. Keeping updated on best security practices and closely monitoring platforms is crucial to mitigating these risks.

Low Liquidity

Some NFTs may have low liquidity in the market, making a quick sale challenging if needed. Investing in less-known NFTs or niche markets may result in lower liquidity compared to more popular assets. Liquidity management is essential to avoid unexpected selling issues.

Diversifying the

NFT Portfolio

Avoiding

Overconcentration

A key strategy for managing risks in NFT investments is diversifying your portfolio. Avoid overconcentration in a single type of NFT or on a specific platform. Investing in a variety of categories, artists, and collections can help reduce the negative impact of poor performance in a specific market area.

Exploring Different NFT Categories

NFTs are not limited to digital artworks. Explore various categories such as games, virtual properties, sports collectibles, and more. Each category has unique market dynamics, and diversifying your portfolio among them can provide additional protection against market fluctuations.

Conducting In-Depth

Research and Analysis

Assessing Artistic and

Conceptual Quality

Not all NFTs are equal. Deepen your research by assessing the artistic and conceptual quality of a work. Consider the importance of the artist in the context of NFTs and look for works that have intrinsic value beyond their current market value.

Analyzing Artist and Project History

Examine the history of the artist or project behind an NFT. Established artists or projects with a solid reputation may offer greater stability and long-term value. Research reviews, past performances, and community involvement for a comprehensive understanding.

Considering Secure Storage

Protecting NFTs from Unauthorized Access

Security is crucial when managing risks in NFT investments. Use secure digital wallets and safeguard your private keys with utmost care. Unauthorized access to your wallet could lead to the irreversible loss of NFTs and associated funds.

Opting for Cold Storage Solutions

Cold storage solutions, such as hardware wallets, provide an additional level of security by separating private keys from internet connections. These options can be particularly useful for investors intending to hold their NFTs for the long term.

Constantly Monitoring

the Market Regular

Updates on Market

Performance

The NFT market is dynamic, with new trends and developments occurring regularly. Constantly monitor market performance, news, and updates related to your collections. Staying abreast of market developments allows you to adapt your investment strategy based on current conditions.

Maintaining Active Communication with the Community

Actively participate in communities related to NFTs. Forums, social media, and discussion platforms provide spaces where investors can share information, discuss new trends, and receive feedback. Active communication with the community can provide valuable insights contributing to risk management.

Establishing Clear

Investment Goals

Defining Realistic

Goals

Before diving into NFT investments, establish clear investment goals. Determine whether you are seeking short-term returns or have a long-term perspective. Defining realistic goals will help you make more considered decisions and avoid impulsive choices during periods of volatility.

Periodically Reassessing the Strategy

The NFT market is in constant evolution. Periodically reassess your investment strategy based on market developments, your personal goals, and financial outlook. An adaptable strategy is essential for effectively managing risks in the long run.

Conclusion: Investing Consciously in NFTs

Managing risks in NFT investments requires a conscious and strategic approach. Understanding specific NFT risks, diversifying your portfolio, conducting in-depth research, considering secure storage, constantly monitoring the market, and establishing clear goals are key elements for successfully navigating the world of NFTs. With prudent risk management, you can maximize growth opportunities and enjoy the benefits offered by this revolutionary digital asset technology.

CHAPTER 11: HIGH-POTENTIAL NFT PROJECTS

In the dynamic world of NFTs, identifying high-potential projects is crucial for anyone looking to make forward-thinking investment decisions. In this chapter, we will explore some NFT projects showing signs of growth and success in the future. Being informed about these emerging initiatives will provide you with a comprehensive overview of opportunities in the vast ecosystem of non- fungible digital assets.

Art Blocks

The Revolution of Programmable Artworks

Art Blocks stands out in the NFT landscape for its innovative approach to programmable artworks. The platform allows artists to create algorithms that generate unique artworks at the moment of purchase. This approach to NFT creation offers a unique experience and could become increasingly popular, attracting both art enthusiasts and investors.

The Sandbox

Build and Monetize Your Virtual World

The Sandbox is a platform that combines the concept of NFTs with the creation of virtual worlds. Users can buy, sell, and own virtual land, create interactive experiences, and monetize their projects. With the growing popularity of metaverses, The Sandbox could emerge as one of the leading platforms for NFTs related to virtual worlds.

Ethernity Chain

NFTs Linked to Celebrities and Iconic Characters

Ethernity Chain focuses on NFTs linked to celebrities and iconic characters. The platform collaborates with personalities from the world of sports, entertainment, and culture to create exclusive collections of NFTs. Investors might see value in collecting NFTs linked to prominent figures, making Ethernity Chain a platform to keep an eye on.

Aavegotchi

Combining DeFi and NFTs in Gaming

Aavegotchi is a project that merges DeFi and NFTs in the context of blockchain games. Users can own creatures called Aavegotchi, which can be used to participate in decentralized finance activities within the game. This synergy between DeFi and NFTs could attract both gamers and cryptocurrency enthusiasts.

Bored Ape Yacht Club

Exclusive Collections of Digital Monkeys

Bored Ape Yacht Club has gained fame for its exclusive collections of NFTs depicting monkeys with unique traits. Owning one of these NFTs grants holders' access to exclusive events and selected communities. The success of Bored Ape Yacht Club could pave the way for additional projects offering exclusive experiences to buyers.

Decentraland

Own, Create, and Monetize Virtual Land

Decentraland is more than an NFT platform; it is a blockchain-based metaverse where users can own, create, and monetize virtual land. The diverse ecosystem of Decentraland, including virtual properties, digital artworks, and more, positions it as a project with significant growth potential.

Rarible

Open and Decentralized NFT Creation and Trading Platform

Rarible is a project that focuses on open and decentralized creation and trading of NFTs. The platform allows artists to mint their NFTs and sell them without going through selection processes. Rarible's user-friendly interface could make it an attractive choice for emerging artists and collectors.

Axie Infinity

Blockchain Games with Unique Creatures

Axie Infinity has secured a prominent place in the world of blockchain games, offering creatures called Axies that users can own, trade, and even battle. The combination of engaging gameplay with ownership of unique digital assets has contributed to the success of Axie Infinity.

CryptoPunks

Pioneers of NFT Collecting

CryptoPunks were among the first to introduce the concept of NFT collecting on the Ethereum blockchain. The small, pixelated images of people, aliens, and creatures have become coveted in the NFT community. Their pioneer status makes them a collection of great interest to investors.

NBA Top Shot

Tokenizing Iconic Moments in NBA

NBA Top Shot has brought NFTs into the sports world, allowing enthusiasts to own and trade iconic moments from the NBA.

Collaboration with a high-profile brand like the NBA could be an indicator of success for future projects seeking to merge the world of NFTs with specific industries.

Sorare

NFTs in the Context of Fantasy Football

Sorare combines the concept of NFTs with fantasy football, allowing users to own and trade cards of soccer players. This combination of two exciting worlds could be replicated in other contexts, paving the way for new and interesting investment opportunities.

Enjin

Integrating NFTs into Games and Apps

Enjin is a platform that provides tools to integrate NFTs into games and applications. Collaborating with various projects, Enjin aims to create an ecosystem where NFTs are used in various digital contexts. Its role in the growth of the NFT ecosystem makes it worthy of attention.

Mintable

Simplified NFT Creation

Mintable stands out for simplifying the process of creating and selling NFTs. Users can easily mint their works, making NFT creation accessible even for emerging artists. Mintable's user-friendly approach could attract a wider audience, contributing to its growth.

WazirX NFT

Exploring NFTs on an Exchange Platform

WazirX NFT is part of the cryptocurrency exchange platform WazirX. It offers users the opportunity to explore and purchase a variety of NFTs directly from the exchange platform. The convenience of accessing NFTs through an established exchange platform could make WazirX NFT an interesting choice for investors.

Theta Network

Video Streaming and NFTs

Theta Network is a project that combines video streaming with NFT technology. Users can earn Theta tokens by watching and sharing video content. The integration of NFTs could open new opportunities in the streaming industry, leading users to seek and own exclusive content.

Conclusion: Strategies for Identifying Future Potential in NFTs

Recognizing high-potential NFT projects requires a combination of research, analysis, and awareness of market trends. There is no magic formula for predicting future success, but keeping an eye on innovative projects, strategic collaborations, and community response can provide indications of long-term project potential. When making investment decisions, it's essential to balance risk with a long-term vision, seeking projects that not only reflect current trends but are also positioned to thrive in an ever-evolving future in the NFT world.

CHAPTER 12: PASSIVE INCOME OPPORTUNITIES WITH NFTS

In the vast ecosystem of NFTs, the opportunity to generate passive income presents itself as an enticing prospect for those looking to grow their wealth without the daily commitment required by other forms of investment. In this chapter, we will explore how NFTs are not only a source of instant gains but also a vehicle for building passive income over time.

Tokenization of Digital Content

Creating Revenue-Generating Digital Assets

One of the primary ways to generate passive income with NFTs is through the tokenization of digital content. Artists, content creators, and holders of intellectual property can transform their works into NFTs and earn royalties every time these are traded on the secondary market. This model allows artists to continue earning even after the initial sale, creating a steady stream of income.

Collecting NFTs with Dividends

Projects Distributing Income to Investors

Some NFT projects implement business models that distribute dividends to investors. Owning specific NFTs from these projects can ensure a consistent return in the form of tokens or cryptocurrencies. These dividends may result from collecting fees, participating in project profits, or other value-generation mechanisms.

NFT Staking

Locking NFTs for Sustainable Returns

The concept of staking, widely used in cryptocurrencies, has been extended to NFTs. Users can "lock" their NFTs in smart contracts to participate in liquidity pools or to support the security and functionality of a platform. In return for their contribution, stakeholders receive returns in the form of new tokens or other rewards, creating a steady stream of passive income.

Delegated NFTs

Delegating Ownership for Returns

The idea of delegating NFT ownership can open new opportunities for passive income. Users can temporarily grant ownership of their NFTs to others or platforms in exchange for a percentage of the profits generated. This practice allows NFT owners to maintain control of the property while benefiting from the earnings generated by its use.

Leasing Virtual Properties

Earning Passive Income by Renting Virtual Land

In metaverses and NFT-based virtual worlds, it's possible to earn passive income by leasing virtual properties. Virtual landowners can lease spaces for events, commercial activities, or other initiatives, earning a regular rental fee. This model resembles the leasing of physical properties but takes place in digital environments.

NFT Investment Funds

Participating in Curated NFT Portfolios

NFT investment funds are emerging as a form of collective investment where investors contribute to a pool of resources managed by experts. These funds can hold a variety of NFTs and generate passive income through active portfolio management. Participating in these funds allows investors to benefit from diversification and the expertise of professional managers.

NFTs in Play-to-

Earn Games Earning

While playing with

NFTs

Blockchain games based on NFTs offer the opportunity to earn while playing. Owning and using specific NFTs in these games can allow users to earn rewards in the form of tokens, in-game items, or other digital assets. This model, known as play-to-earn, creates a dynamic where the enjoyment of the game is combined with the possibility of passive income.

NFTs Linked to

Smart Contracts

Automating Income

Generation

NFTs based on smart contracts can be programmed to generate automatic income. For example, a digital artwork could be designed to pay a percentage of proceeds every time it is resold. This approach allows artists to create a continuous income stream, and buyers to participate in potential future profits.

NFTs in Decentralized

Finance (DeFi) Harnessing

DeFi Opportunities

The integration of NFTs into decentralized finance (DeFi) opens

the door to many passive income opportunities. Users can use their NFTs as collateral in loans and earn interest or participate in liquidity pools to get returns on their participation. This synergy between NFTs and DeFi creates a diverse range of income-generating opportunities.

NFT Marketplaces with

Affiliate Programs Earning

Through Affiliate Marketing

Some NFT marketplaces offer affiliate programs that allow users to earn commissions by promoting and facilitating transactions. Affiliates can receive a percentage of the fees generated by transactions resulting from their involvement. This model encourages active promotion of the marketplace, creating a stream of income for those participating in the affiliate program.

NFTs Linked to Exclusive Events and Content

Monetizing Participation in Exclusive Events and Content

Some NFT projects offer content or access to exclusive events as part of the purchase of an NFT. Owning such NFTs not only provides an exclusive advantage but can also be monetized through participation in events or the sale of access privileges. This model relies on scarcity and exclusivity to generate added value.

Conclusion: Building a Sustainable Income Stream

The opportunity for passive income with NFTs is a fascinating aspect of this innovative technology. However, it's crucial to note that, like any form of investment, success in generating a lasting income stream requires careful strategy, thorough research, and a deep understanding of the market.

Experimenting with different forms of passive income with NFTs and adapting one's strategy based on industry trends can help investors build a diversified and sustainable portfolio over time. The key is to be open to innovation, monitor new opportunities, and proactively adapt to changes in the NFT market to maximize the potential for passive income in the long term.

CHAPTER 13: THE EXPLOSION OF NFT COLLECTIONS

In the dynamic landscape of NFTs, the rise of collections plays a crucial role in shaping the future of the market. This chapter serves as an essential guide for those wishing to identify hidden opportunities and capitalize on them. We will explore the dynamics of NFT collections, analyzing how to identify growing projects and seize emerging trends.

Emerging Trends in NFT Collections

The Importance of Recognizing Current Trends

To fully capitalize on the explosion of NFT collections, understanding emerging trends in the market is crucial. Staying updated is essential due to the rapid emergence and popularity gain of new ideas and concepts. Trends such as programmable art, NFTs linked to real-time events, and collaborations with well-known brands can offer unique opportunities for investors.

Programmable and Generative Art

Exploring the Future of Digital Artistic Expression

Programmable and generative art has emerged as a significant trend in NFT collections. Artists using algorithms to create unique and ever-changing artworks are attracting the attention of digital art enthusiasts and investors. This combination of creativity and technology offers a unique experience in the world of NFT collections.

NFTs Linked to Real-Time Events

Immediacy as a Key Element

Collections of NFTs linked to real-time events are gaining popularity for their unique and immediate nature. Projects capturing significant moments in real-time, such as sports events, concerts, or culturally resonant situations, can have a significant impact on the market. Investors keen on capturing these fleeting moments can benefit from growing demand.

Collaborations with Brands and Celebrities Joining Forces to Maximize Appeal

Collaborations between NFT projects, well-known brands, and celebrities are a trend that continues to gain momentum. The participation of prominent figures in NFT projects can significantly increase the visibility and appeal of collections. Investors identifying projects supported by strategic collaborations can enjoy a significant boost in long-term value.

Limited Edition Collections and Scarcity Creating a Sense of Exclusivity

Limited edition NFT collections characterized by scarcity are succeeding among collectors. Creating a limited quantity of digital artworks or virtual objects increases the perception of their value and exclusivity. Identifying projects that leverage the scarcity strategy can be an effective way to build a portfolio of NFT collections capable of maintaining or increasing their value over time.

Collections Linked to Virtual
Worlds and Metaverses The
Intersection of NFTs and Virtual
Worlds

Collections of NFTs linked to virtual worlds and metaverses are gaining ground. Virtual properties, in- game items, and other digital assets within blockchain-based virtual worlds are becoming areas of interest for collectors. Investing in collections linked to these digital experiences can open up new opportunities for earnings and interaction.

Charity NFT

Projects

Collecting for a

Good Cause

Charity NFT projects are emerging as a significant trend, combining the passion for digital collections with philanthropy. Collecting NFTs through projects that allocate a portion of sales to charitable causes can not only bring personal satisfaction but also create long-term value. Investors with an ethical perspective may find these collections particularly attractive.

NFTs Linked to Multimedia Content

Beyond Art: Growing Multimedia Collections

Beyond digital art, NFT collections linked to multimedia content are gaining ground. Films, music, podcasts, and more are now subjects of tokenization. Investors attentive to projects that extend beyond the traditional scope of digital art may discover new and exciting collection opportunities.

Technological Innovations in

NFT Collections Exploring the

Impact of Technology on

Collections

Technological innovations, such as the integration of augmented reality (AR) and virtual reality (VR) into NFT collections, are creating unique experiences for collectors. Identifying projects that embrace new technologies can be an indicator of growth and innovation in the world of NFTs.

NFT Collections Linked to Exclusive Experiences Beyond Mere Ownership: The Exclusivity of Experience

Some NFT collections go beyond mere ownership of digital artwork, offering exclusive experiences to holders. Access to special events, meetings with artists, or participation in interactive projects are integral parts of these collections. Investors interested in unique experiences may find added value in projects that go beyond the traditional collection model.

Conclusion: Strategies to Identify Successful Collections

Recognizing opportunities in NFT collections requires a combination of market sensitivity, in-depth research, and a clear understanding of emerging trends. Investors can adopt strategies such as portfolio diversification, participation in active communities, and constant monitoring of new proposals to identify successful projects. Remaining flexible and open to innovation is essential in the dynamic world of NFTs, where opportunities can manifest in unexpected ways. With a visionary outlook and a careful assessment of trends, investors can maximize their potential for success in the growth of NFT collections.

CHAPTER 14:
GETTING READY FOR
THE FUTURE OF NFTS

The world of NFTs is a fertile ground for innovation and change, constantly evolving to meet the needs and trends of the digital market. In this chapter, we will explore emerging trends in the world of NFTs and how to prepare for the future, ensuring to stay ahead in the rapidly changing market.

Integration of NFTs

into Traditional Areas

Merging the Digital and the

Traditional

One emerging trend is the increasingly close integration of NFTs into traditional areas of society. Experiments with NFTs are taking place in sectors such as traditional art, education, the music industry, and much more. Investors and NFT enthusiasts should keep an eye on these innovations as they can open new horizons and increase the spread and acceptance of NFTs in mainstream culture.

NFTs in Virtual and

Augmented Reality Expanding

Experiences with New

Technologies

The integration of NFTs into virtual reality (VR) and augmented reality (AR) is gaining momentum. This synergy offers new ways for NFT holders to experience their collections, allowing them to interact with their assets in entirely new ways. The ability to view digital artworks in the context of the real world through VR or AR creates an engaging and interactive experience.

Evolved NFTs and Smart

Contracts Towards More

Complex Smart Contracts

The technology of smart contracts, fundamental to NFTs, is expected to evolve. The next generation of smart contracts may introduce more complex elements, allowing, for example, automatic exchanges of resources or decentralized governance mechanisms within collections. Being aware of these innovations is essential for those looking to stay at the forefront of the industry.

Environmental Sustainability in NFTs

Addressing Concerns about Environmental Impact

Environmental sustainability has become a central concern in the NFT ecosystem. Many projects are exploring solutions to mitigate the environmental impact of cryptocurrency mining associated with NFTs. Sustainability-oriented investors should look for projects adopting eco-friendly practices and innovative solutions to reduce environmental impact.

NFTs in the Education

and Training Sectors

Transforming Learning

through Tokenization

NFTs are making their way into the education and training sectors, revolutionizing the tokenization of diplomas, certificates, and educational content. Monitoring how NFTs integrate into these sectors can be crucial, as new investment and participation opportunities may emerge.

Evolution of NFT

Business Models New

Approaches to Generate

Income

Business models related to NFTs are evolving. Developers and entrepreneurs are exploring new approaches to generate income, such as introducing subscriptions, memberships, and other monetization mechanisms within NFT collections. Being aware of these innovations can help investors assess the long-term sustainability and profitability of an NFT project.

NFTs Linked to Digital Identity

Security and Authentication through NFTs

The tokenization of digital identity is emerging as a promising application of NFTs. Using blockchain to ensure security and authentication, NFTs could become digital keys for secure access to online services, documents, and personal information. Understanding how NFTs influence digital identity can be fundamental in the context of growing digitization.

NFTs and Artificial Intelligence

Synthesis of Two Technological Revolutions

The integration of NFTs with artificial intelligence (AI) offers new opportunities and challenges. Projects that combine these two technological revolutions can create unique experiences and automate processes within NFT collections. Being aware of how these technologies merge can provide insight into the future potential of NFTs.

Active Participation in

NFT Communities Active

Communities as Drivers of

Innovation

NFT communities are playing an increasingly crucial role in shaping the future of the industry. Investors and enthusiasts who actively participate in communities can gain valuable insights, identify new projects early on, and contribute to the development of ethical standards and sustainable practices in the NFT ecosystem.

NFT Regulation

Adapting to an Evolving Regulatory Landscape

NFT regulation is a rapidly evolving aspect of the industry. Investors should stay updated on new laws and regulations that may influence the buying and selling of NFTs. Adapting to an evolving regulatory landscape is crucial to ensuring secure and law-compliant transactions.

Conclusion: Being Ready for Continuous Innovation

Preparing for the future of NFTs requires a proactive approach and a willingness to adapt to continuous innovation in the industry. Carefully monitoring emerging trends, actively participating in communities, being open to new applications of NFTs, and understanding technological evolution are all key elements to stay ahead in the dynamic world of NFTs. Being ready to embrace change is the key to capitalizing on future opportunities and maintaining a leadership position in the NFT market.

CHAPTER 15:
ESSENTIAL TOOLS
FOR NFT INVESTORS

Being a successful investor in the world of NFTs requires not only a thorough understanding of the market but also the effective use of the right tools. In this chapter, we will explore the essential tools needed to monitor, manage, and optimize an NFT portfolio, ensuring that investors can make informed decisions and maximize their earning potential.

NFT Marketplace

Platforms Exploring

Buying and Selling

Options

NFT marketplace platforms are the starting point for every investor. Platforms such as OpenSea, Rarible, and Foundation offer a wide variety of NFTs for sale. Being familiar with the features and fees of these platforms is essential to navigate the market and find investment opportunities.

NFT Market

Trackers

Monitoring Market

Movements

NFT market trackers provide a real-time overview of market trends and movements. Tools like NonFungible and CryptoSlam allow investors to monitor statistics, transactions, and trading volumes of specific collections, gaining an in-depth understanding of market dynamics.

Secure Crypto

Wallets Protecting

Your Digital Assets

Security is a priority when investing in NFTs. A secure crypto wallet, such as MetaMask or Ledger Nano S, is essential to protect digital assets. Ensuring the use of wallets with robust security measures and carefully storing private keys is crucial to avoid hacking risks or asset loss.

Crypto Tax

Calculators

Managing Tax

Implications

NFT transactions can have complex tax implications. Using a crypto tax calculator, such as CoinTracker or TokenTax, can simplify the management of taxes associated with buying and selling NFTs, ensuring compliance with tax regulations.

Technical Analysis

Tools Assessing

Market Trends

Technical analysis tools, like TradingView, are valuable for investors wanting to assess market trends and make informed decisions. Analyzing charts, identifying support and resistance levels, and using technical indicators can help predict future market movements.

Community and Social

Media Monitoring Staying

Connected with the

Community

Participating in NFT communities on platforms like Discord and Twitter can provide valuable information. Monitoring discussions, new releases, and expert opinions can be helpful to stay updated on the latest developments and identify new investment opportunities.

On-Chain Metrics Analysis

Exploring Data Directly from the Blockchain

On-chain metrics analysis provides data directly from the blockchain, allowing investors to assess the health and vitality of an NFT collection. Tools like Dune Analytics offer detailed metrics on usage and transactions in blockchain-based collections.

NFT Discovery

Services

Finding New

Opportunities

NFT discovery services, such as NFTb.io or Mintable, can help investors find new collection opportunities. These services allow exploration of emerging projects, tracking the latest releases, and discovering rising artists or collectors.

Tokenization Platforms

Exploring Different Forms of Digital Assets

Tokenization platforms allow investors to explore different forms of digital assets beyond art, such as tokens tied to events, multimedia content, or virtual properties. Platforms like Mintable offer options for creating and exchanging a wide range of digital tokens.

NFT Creation Tools

Creating and Managing Your Collections

Investors wishing to create their own NFT collections can use creation tools like Rarible or Mintable. These tools make it easy to upload, create, and manage their tokenized digital works.

Conclusion: Empower Yourself with the Right Tools

Successful NFT investors are those who fully leverage the tools at their disposal. The combination of marketplace platforms, market trackers, secure wallets, and other specialized tools can provide investors with the insight and control needed to navigate the complex and dynamic world of NFTs. Investing time in understanding and effectively using these tools is an investment in oneself, enabling individuals to make informed decisions and maximize earning potential in the ever-evolving NFT market.

CHAPTER 16: NFT IN THE WORLD OF DIGITAL ART

The fusion of NFTs and digital art represents a revolution in the artistic ecosystem, opening new frontiers for artists and collectors. In this chapter, we will delve into how NFT technology has transformed how artists can monetize their talent and how collectors can own unique digital artworks, giving rise to a renewed landscape in digital art.

Unleashing Creative Potential:

Artists and Tokenization The Digital

Ownership Revolution

For artists, tokenization through NFTs represents a revolution in digital ownership. In the past, sharing digital artworks often meant losing control over their distribution and reproduction. With NFTs, artists can ensure the scarcity of their works, attribute ownership rights, and receive a percentage of subsequent sales, allowing them to monetize their talent more fairly and directly.

Creating Scarcity in the

Digital World Rarity as a

Value Factor

One of the key innovations introduced by NFTs is the

ability to create "rare" digital artworks. The blockchain, with its immutable nature, allows artists to limit the quantity of available NFTs for a particular work. This artificial scarcity can significantly increase the perceived and real value of the artwork, making it more desirable for collectors.

Democratization of

Access to Art Inclusion

and Accessibility

Thanks to NFTs, access to digital art has democratized. Emerging artists now have the opportunity to get noticed without the need for a traditional art gallery or intermediaries. Collecting digital art is no longer reserved for an elite audience; anyone with access to a blockchain can participate and appreciate digital art.

Direct Monetization

for Artists Earning

from Every Resale

One of the revolutionary aspects of NFTs is the ability to earn directly from the subsequent exchanges of their works. Thanks to smart contracts, artists can receive a predefined percentage from each resale, creating a continuous source of income. This innovative model overturns the traditional system where artists received a one-time payment for their work and did not benefit from future appreciations.

Exploring New Forms of

Artistic Expression Beyond

Traditional Conventions

NFTs have opened doors to new forms of digital artistic expression. Artists experimenting with programmable art, generative art, and the integration of multimedia elements can find fertile ground in the world of NFTs to explore and share their creativity in innovative ways.

The Birth of Digital

Collectors Digitally

Owning, Physically

Collecting

NFTs have given rise to a new category of collectors: digital collectors. Owning unique digital artworks has become a way for art enthusiasts to showcase their taste and interest in digital culture. Some digital collectors extend their passion into the physical world by printing and framing their NFT artworks.

Opportunities for Art Galleries

Challenges and Opportunities for Traditional Institutions

Traditional art galleries are experiencing the challenges and opportunities offered by NFTs. The tokenization of artworks can open new avenues for exhibiting and selling digital works, but it also raises questions about managing physical pieces. Art spaces embracing NFT technology can tap into new markets and reach a broader audience.

NFTs as a Narrative

Element Weaving

Stories and Digital

Works

NFTs allow artists to weave stories and narratives with their digital artworks. By connecting related NFTs, artists can create a unique and engaging narrative that goes beyond the individual piece, offering collectors a richer and interconnected experience.

Sustainability in

Digital Art Addressing

Environmental

Concerns

Environmental sustainability is a growing concern in the art industry. NFTs, based on blockchain, have faced criticism for their environmental impact due to cryptocurrency mining. Some artists and platforms are exploring sustainable solutions and eco-friendly practices to mitigate this issue.

The Future of

Digital Art with

NFTs Exploring New

Frontiers

The future of digital art with NFTs is full of potential. The evolution of blockchain technologies, the integration of augmented and virtual reality, along with new forms of tokenization, promise to take digital art to new frontiers. Artists and collectors are called to be pioneers in this journey, contributing to defining the future of digital art.

Conclusion: A New Digital Renaissance

The fusion of NFTs and digital art is shaping a new digital renaissance, redefining the very nature of art and its consumption. Artists are emancipated, collectors are digitally savvy, and the possibilities for creative expression are virtually limitless. Through NFTs, we are witnessing a paradigm shift in digital art that promises to leave a lasting imprint on the digital cultural history.

CHAPTER 17: CRYPTO ART AND ITS EXPLOSIVE GROWTH

The world of Crypto Art has experienced explosive growth in recent years, radically transforming how artists create, share, and monetize their digital artworks. In this chapter, we will explore the rapid expansion of Crypto Art, examining how artists and collectors are embracing this form of digital artistic expression and the financial opportunities associated with it.

Crypto Art: A Revolution in

Artistic Expression The Dawn

of a New Era

Crypto Art marks the beginning of a new era in digital artistic expression. Based on blockchain and supported by smart contracts, this art form allows artists to create unique digital works, ensuring their authenticity and enabling tokenization for sale.

The Role of Blockchain in

Digital Art Transparency

and Security

Blockchain plays a fundamental role in Crypto Art by providing transparency and security. The immutable registration of works on a blockchain eliminates the risk of counterfeiting and ensures that the provenance of each piece is clear and verifiable.

NFTs as the Key to

Scarcity Creating

Value Through

Exclusivity

NFTs, whether fungible or not, are the key to introducing scarcity into digital art. The ability to limit the quantity of tokens associated with a digital artwork creates a sense of exclusivity, increasing its value both in artistic and financial terms.

Artists and the

Digital Revolution

From Unknown to

Icon

Crypto Art has allowed previously unknown artists to emerge as digital icons. The democratization of access to digital art has opened doors for emerging talents, enabling them to be noticed without the traditional barriers of the art industry.

Digital Collectors and New

Forms of Ownership Digital Art

as an Asset

Digital collectors are embracing Crypto Art as a new form of ownership and investment. Owning an NFT represents not only access to digital art but also possession of a digital asset that can appreciate over time.

The Explosive Growth of the

Crypto Art Market Success in

Numbers

The Crypto Art market has experienced explosive growth, with transactions reaching impressive figures. Digital auction houses like Christie's and Sotheby's have started to include Crypto Artworks in their events, confirming institutional recognition and the financial value of these digital creations.

Financial Opportunities for Artists

Earning Beyond the Initial Sale

Crypto Art offers unique financial opportunities for artists. In addition to the initial sale of a work, artists can earn continuously through royalties associated with NFTs, receiving a percentage from each resale of their work.

NFT Platforms: Creative

Labs for Artists Creation,

Exchange, and Community

NFT platforms like OpenSea, Rarible, and Foundation have become true creative labs for artists. These digital spaces allow artists to create, trade, and interact with a broad community of collectors and enthusiasts.

Crypto Art and

Popular Culture

From Memes to

High Fashion

Crypto Art has transcended the boundaries of popular culture. Digital artworks based on memes, viral images, and even in digital fashion are becoming integral parts of contemporary culture, highlighting the impact of this art form on society.

Challenges and

Criticisms Addressing

Concerns and

Criticisms

Despite its success, Crypto Art also faces challenges and criticisms. Environmental concerns related to the energy used by the blockchain and questions about speculation in the Crypto Art market are topics that require careful attention.

Crypto Art and

Charity Using Technology for Good

Some artists and platforms are using Crypto Art for charitable purposes, donating a portion of the proceeds from sales to social or environmental causes. This combination of art and charity underscores the potential positive impact of Crypto Art on society.

The Promising Future of Crypto Art Innovations on the Horizon

The future of Crypto Art looks promising, with ample room for innovations. The integration of new technologies, such as augmented reality and virtual reality, could open up new creative possibilities, further redefining the landscape of Crypto Art.

Conclusion: Crypto Art as a Cultural Force

The explosive growth of the Crypto Art world is more than a trend; it has become a cultural force that has redefined the very concept of art. Artists are free to explore new forms of expression, collectors are embracing digital art, and blockchain technology has made this revolution possible. Crypto Art is not just an artistic phenomenon but a reflection of our digital age and its infinite possibilities.

CHAPTER 18: CRYPTOPUNKS - ICONS OF THE NFT WORLD

CryptoPunks, undoubtedly, have become legendary icons in the vast landscape of NFTs. These eccentric and distinctive pixel art creations are not just digital collectibles; they have taken on the role of status symbols in the world of Non-Fungible Tokens. In this chapter, we will examine the history of CryptoPunks, their revolutionary impact, and how they have become true icons in the NFT market.

The Genesis of CryptoPunks

The Dawn of Digital Art on the Blockchain

In the distant year 2017, Matt Hall and John Watkinson, founders of Larva Labs, decided to create 10,000 unique pixelated characters, each different from the others, and named them CryptoPunks. This move represented one of the early experiments in using blockchain for digital art, leveraging Ethereum technology and smart contracts to ensure authenticity and ownership of the works.

The Originality of Each

CryptoPunk 10,000

Pixelated Uniqueness

The distinctive feature of CryptoPunks lies in their originality. Each CryptoPunk is a unique, non- replicable character. The combination of features such as hair, eyes, mouth, and accessories differ from one punk to another, creating a collection of unique and unrepeatable digital artworks.

Free Distribution and the

Birth of the Market From

Gift to NFT Market Icon

Initially, Larva Labs distributed CryptoPunks for free to anyone with an Ethereum address. This act of generosity became a turning point in the history of NFTs, with CryptoPunks later gaining value in the NFT exchange market.

The Rise to Success

From Niche Phenomenon to Mainstream Icon

The popularity of CryptoPunks has experienced exponential growth. What started as a niche phenomenon within the crypto community quickly transformed into a mainstream icon in the world of NFTs. CryptoPunks have captured the attention of collectors, investors, and digital art enthusiasts worldwide.

The Revolutionary

Impact Redefining

Digital Ownership

CryptoPunks have had a revolutionary impact on the perception of digital ownership. They have demonstrated that a digital artwork can be owned and traded like any physical asset, utilizing blockchain to ensure ownership and scarcity.

CryptoPunks as

Status Symbols Status

Symbols in the NFT

World

Today, owning a CryptoPunk has become a status symbol in the world of NFTs. The rarity and originality of these pixelated characters confer a unique prestige upon their owners. Some

CryptoPunks have become true status trophies, marking the position of their owners within the NFT enthusiast community.

Sales Records

Stratospheri

c Values

The NFT exchange market has witnessed impressive sales records related to CryptoPunks. Some of these pixelated characters have reached stratospheric values, with figures nearing millions of dollars. These record-breaking sales have attracted the attention of the general public, further solidifying the reputation of CryptoPunks as prestigious assets.

Cultural and

Mainstream Impact

From Niche to Digital

Pop Pharaohs

CryptoPunks have surpassed the boundaries of the crypto community and NFT enthusiasts, infiltrating popular culture. Their presence has been noted in television programs, fashion magazines, and countless online articles, transforming them from a niche phenomenon into digital pop pharaohs.

CryptoPunks as

Autonomous Art Form

Exploring New Definitions

of Art

CryptoPunks have brought the issue of defining autonomous art to the forefront. These pixelated characters, without a traditional artistic context, challenge conventional conceptions of what constitutes art, opening new perspectives on what can be considered artwork in the digital age.

The CryptoPunks

Community Unity

and Fun in Diversity

The community of CryptoPunk owners has become a phenomenon in itself. Members share a sense of belonging, united by the diversity of their pixelated characters. Events, initiatives, and even in- person meetings have become integral parts of this unique community.

Criticisms and Controversies

Debates on Exclusivity and Accessibility

With the exponential growth of CryptoPunks, debates and controversies have also emerged. Some critics raise concerns about the exclusivity and lack of accessibility of these digital artworks, emphasizing challenges related to fairness in the world of NFTs.

The Future of

CryptoPunks New

Frontiers and

Challenges

The future of CryptoPunks is open to new frontiers and challenges. With the continued development of the NFT market, the evolution of blockchain technology, and the growing interest from artists and collectors, CryptoPunks will continue to shape the future of digital art and inspire future generations of artists and NFT enthusiasts.

Conclusion: Undisputed Icons

CryptoPunks have become not only iconic but undisputed icons in the world of NFTs. Their story is a journey through the evolution of digital ownership, rarity, and value in the digital era. As pioneers of a new artistic paradigm, CryptoPunks will continue to influence the landscape of digital art and inspire future generations of artists and NFT enthusiasts.

CHAPTER 19: NFTS IN THE GAMING WORLD

NFTs are opening new dimensions in the gaming industry, redefining the concept of virtual ownership, and creating unique opportunities for players to own, trade, and monetize virtual assets within games. In this chapter, we will explore how Non-Fungible Tokens are revolutionizing the gaming world, influencing how players interact with their favorite virtual universes.

Transformation of Virtual

Ownership Beyond

Temporary Possession

Traditionally, players only owned virtual assets within the game context, with the possibility of losing or selling them limited to the specific gaming platform. NFTs are transforming this dynamic, allowing players to permanently and transferably own virtual assets through the blockchain.

Creating, Owning, and

Trading Unique Items

Customization and

Exchange of Goods

NFTs enable players to create, own, and trade unique items within games. Whether it's character skins, rare weapons, or other customization elements, each item can become a unique

NFT, giving tangible and unique value to virtual elements.

NFT Markets

Within Games

Creating Economic

Ecosystems

Games are increasingly integrating NFT markets within their platforms. These markets allow players to buy, sell, and trade virtual goods using NFTs, thereby creating dynamic economic ecosystems within games. The introduction of mechanisms like smart contracts enables secure and traceable transactions.

Monetization Opportunities

for Players Earning Through

Skill and Dedication

Thanks to NFTs, players can monetize their skills and dedication in games. Rare items and virtual resources can be traded on NFT markets, allowing players to earn cryptocurrencies or other digital assets in exchange for their in-game achievements.

NFT Performance-Linked

Tokens Recognizing and

Rewarding Performance

Some games are introducing NFTs linked to performance, rewarding players for their achievements and successes. These tokens serve as digital recognitions and can be used to unlock special content, gain privileges, or participate in exclusive in-game events.

Players as True

Owners Sovereign

Over Virtual

Properties

NFTs transform players into true owners of their virtual resources. Owning an NFT associated with an in-game item means being the true sovereign of that asset, with the ability to decide how to use it, whether to keep it or sell it to another player.

Interoperability Between Games

Beyond Platform Limitations

NFTs pave the way for interoperability between different games. An NFT-owned item in one game could be used or traded in another, overcoming traditional platform-related limitations. This offers players an unprecedented level of flexibility and diversification.

Creating and Trading User-

Generated Content Active

Participation in Creation

NFTs allow players to create and trade user-generated content (UGC) more dynamically and securely. Objects, skins, and other user-created items can be tokenized and traded with other players through NFT markets, offering earning opportunities for the creative minds within the gaming community.

The Role of Smart Contracts

in Gaming Security and

Automation in Transactions

Smart contracts play a crucial role in implementing NFTs in gaming. These contracts automate transactions, ensuring security and transparency. They also enable the programming of specific rules, such as royalties for developers when an NFT is resold on the secondary market.

Challenges and

Controversies

Balancing Game and

Monetization

Despite the benefits, the integration of NFTs in gaming raises some challenges and controversies. Developers must balance monetization with the gaming experience, avoiding creating inequalities among players due to NFT resources.

The Future of NFTs in

Gaming Innovations and

Developments Ahead

The future of NFTs in gaming looks promising, with constant innovations and developments. Broader integration of NFTs, the evolution of blockchain platforms, and the growing interest of players promise to further redefine the gaming experience.

Conclusion: A New Level of Possibilities

NFTs are taking the gaming world to a new level of possibilities. Virtual ownership becomes tangible through tokenization, and players become protagonists of their gaming experience. With the continuous evolution of this technology, the boundary between the virtual and real worlds will continue to blur, opening unexplored paths for the gaming industry and its global community of players.

CHAPTER 20: TOKENIZATION OF REAL ASSETS THROUGH NFTS

The tokenization of real assets through Non-Fungible Tokens (NFTs) represents one of the most innovative and revolutionary applications in transforming the concept of physical ownership. In this chapter, we will explore how tokenization is radically changing the way we own and invest in real assets, such as real estate and land.

The Revolution of Physical

Ownership Beyond

Traditional Real Estate

Ownership

Ownership of physical assets, like homes and land, has long been constrained by complex bureaucratic processes and high transaction costs. Tokenization through NFTs offers an alternative, opening new horizons in the management and investment of physical properties.

What is Tokenization of

Real Assets? Representing

Ownership on the

Blockchain

Tokenization of real assets involves the digital representation of ownership of a physical asset through the issuance of NFTs on a blockchain. Each NFT represents a specific share of that asset and can be transferred and traded securely and transparently.

Blockchain as a Digital Real

Estate Registry Replacing

Traditional Registers

The blockchain serves as a digital real estate registry, eliminating the need for centrally managed traditional registers. Ownership information is immutable and easily accessible, reducing the risks of fraud and simplifying property transfer processes.

Accessibility and Democracy in

Real Estate Investment Universal

Participation

Tokenization makes real estate investment more accessible and democratic. Fractions of ownership represented by NFTs allow investors to participate in real estate projects even with more limited budgets, opening doors to a broader range of participants.

Fractionalization of Properties

Creating Opportunities for Small Investors

Thanks to tokenization, it is possible to fractionate a property into multiple NFTs, enabling small investors to purchase shares of the property. This fractionalization makes real estate investments more flexible and suitable for various portfolio sizes.

Liquidity and Secondary

Market Transforming Real

Estate into a Liquid Asset

Tokenization brings liquidity to real estate investments, allowing investors to trade their ownership shares on secondary NFT markets. This liquidity offers flexibility in divestment or acquiring new opportunities without waiting for traditional transactions.

Security and Transparency in Transactions

Smart Contracts for Secure Transactions

Smart contracts on the blockchain automatically and securely manage transactions related to the tokenization of real assets. Contractual conditions, such as property transfers or rent distributions, are transparently encoded, reducing the risk of disputes.

Cost and Transaction Time

Reduction Optimizing the

Transaction Process

Tokenization of real assets significantly reduces the costs and time associated with traditional real estate transactions. By eliminating intermediaries and streamlining bureaucratic processes, tokenization makes the buying and selling cycle more efficient.

Tokenization in the Real

Estate Sector Pioneering

Projects and Successes

The real estate sector has already witnessed pioneering tokenization projects with remarkable success. Commercial properties, residential units, and land have been fractionated into NFTs, creating new investment opportunities and showcasing the potential of tokenization in the industry.

Challenges and

Criticisms Security

and Legal Risks

Despite the advantages, tokenization of real assets presents some challenges. Transaction security and legal risks related to registration and contractual execution require particular attention and the evolution of regulations.

The Future of Tokenization

of Real Assets Expansion

and Integration

The future of tokenization of real assets looks to be one of increasing expansion and integration. With the evolution of blockchain technology, the adoption of regulatory standards, and the growing interest from investors, tokenization could become the norm in the real estate sector.

Conclusion: Transforming Physical Ownership

The tokenization of real assets through NFTs represents a radical transformation in the conception of physical ownership. The blockchain becomes the new playing field for real estate investment, offering new opportunities and redefining industry parameters. With the acceleration of adoption and continuous innovation, tokenization could be the key to making real estate more accessible, transparent, and dynamic for everyone.

CHAPTER 21: NFTS IN THE MUSIC INDUSTRY

The world of music is undergoing an unprecedented revolution thanks to the increasing adoption of Non-Fungible Tokens (NFTs). In this chapter, we will explore how artists are using NFTs to transform music distribution, engage fans in innovative ways, and create new sources of income in the ever-evolving music industry.

The Evolution of the Music Landscape

Challenges and Opportunities in the Digital World

The music industry has faced a series of challenges in transitioning to the digital era, including piracy and new distribution models. NFTs offer new opportunities for artists to establish stronger connections with fans, overcoming traditional challenges in the music industry.

Creating Musical Works as NFTs

Transforming Music into Unique Digital Assets

Artists can now create and distribute musical works as NFTs, transforming each track into a unique and authenticated digital asset on the blockchain. This tokenization provides fans with the chance to own a tangible part of the music they love.

Engaging Fans through

NFTs Exclusive and

Interactive Experiences

NFTs allow artists to engage fans through exclusive and interactive experiences. Owning a musical NFT can unlock special privileges, such as access to exclusive virtual concerts, virtual backstage passes, or behind-the-scenes content.

Creating Scarcity and

Exclusivity Adding

Value to Musical

Content

Tokenization automatically creates scarcity and exclusivity around musical content. Artists can limit the availability of certain musical NFTs, giving them a unique value and creating a dynamic of supply and demand among fans.

Revolutionizing

Music Distribution

Surpassing Traditional

Intermediaries

NFTs offer artists the chance to distribute their music directly to fans, bypassing traditional intermediaries such as record labels. This decentralization puts artists at the forefront of creative control and distribution decisions.

New Sources of Income

for Artists Creative and

Sustainable Monetization

NFTs open new income sources for artists. In addition to direct sales of musical NFTs, artists can earn through automatic royalties every time an NFT is resold on the secondary market, ensuring continuous monetization over time.

Launching Exclusive Collections

Exploring New Launch Models

Artists can launch exclusive collections of musical NFTs, creating anticipation and interest among fans. These collections may include special album versions, unreleased tracks, limited editions, and more, offering fans the opportunity to own something truly unique.

NFTs as a Musical

Experience Beyond

the Simple Audio

Track

Artists can use NFTs to offer fans a more comprehensive musical experience. In addition to audio tracks, NFTs can include visual elements, exclusive lyrics, digital artwork, and more, creating an engaging multimedia experience.

Collaboration between

Artists and Collectors Unique

Connections between Creator

and Fan

Tokenization opens the door to unique collaborations between artists and collectors. Artists can create NFTs in collaboration with their fans, actively involving them in the creative process and establishing deeper connections.

Challenges

and Criticisms

Scalability and

Accessibility

Despite the opportunities, NFTs in the music industry face challenges related to scalability and accessibility. Managing demand, creating inclusive experiences, and reducing technological barriers are important challenges to overcome.

The Future of the Music

Industry with NFTs

Innovations and New

Models

The future of the music industry with NFTs promises innovations and new models. Increasing adoption, the evolution of blockchain platforms, and the entry of prominent artists herald a radical transformation in the creation, distribution, and enjoyment of music.

Conclusion: A Harmonic Revolution

NFTs are revolutionizing the music industry, transforming the distribution and consumption of musical content. Artists can now connect more directly and creatively with their fans, offering unique experiences and redefining the concept of value in digital music. With the relentless growth of this trend, the music industry is poised for a new era of innovation, decentralization, and meaningful connections between artists and music enthusiasts.

CHAPTER 22: REGULATION AND LAWS ON NFTS

With the rapid growth of the Non-Fungible Tokens (NFT) market, the issue of regulation has become a crucial component to ensure stability, security, and investor trust. In this chapter, we will examine current and future laws that could influence the world of NFTs, outlining the challenges and opportunities that regulation brings.

The Current Legal

Environment for NFTs An

Evolving Territory

Currently, the legal landscape for NFTs is evolving and varies significantly from jurisdiction to jurisdiction. Many countries are still trying to adapt their existing laws to address the peculiarities of NFTs, while others are developing new specific regulations.

Challenges of Regulation

A New and Dynamic Sector

One of the main challenges in regulating NFTs is the dynamic and innovative nature of the sector. Laws must adapt quickly to technological changes and new ways of exchanging and using NFTs, making the regulatory process a complex endeavor.

Identification of

Involved Parties

Owners, Creators,

Investors

Regulation must address the issue of identifying and assigning responsibilities to the various actors involved in the world of NFTs. These include NFT owners, creators of tokenized content, and investors participating in the market.

Intellectual Property and

Copyright Protection and

Management of Digital

Works

The tokenization of artworks, music, and other content raises questions about intellectual property and copyright. Regulation must ensure adequate protection for artists and investors, clearly defining digital property rights.

Investor Protection

Ensuring Safety and Transparency

Regulation of NFTs must place a strong emphasis on investor protection. Transparency in transactions, security of exchange platforms, and management of financial information are all crucial elements to ensure a safe investment environment.

Taxation of NFT

Investments Clear

Tax Rules

The taxation of NFT investments is another important aspect of regulation. Clear tax rules must be established to ensure that investors are aware of the tax obligations related to NFT transactions.

Combating Illicit Activities

Preventing Money Laundering and Fraud

Regulation must also address the risk of illicit activities such as money laundering and fraud related to NFTs. Implementing anti-money laundering measures and security checks is essential to maintain market integrity.

Standardization and

Interoperability Creating

a Common Regulatory

Basis

The adoption of common standards and protocols for NFTs can simplify regulation, creating a common regulatory basis that crosses borders. Interoperability between different blockchains and protocols can promote more effective and uniform regulation.

International

Perspective

Collaboration between

Jurisdictions

Given the global nature of NFTs, regulation must also be addressed internationally. Collaboration between jurisdictions can help avoid legal conflicts and promote global standards in the NFT market.

Future Legislative

Developments

Adapting to

Innovation

The future of legislative developments on NFTs is uncertain but promising. Authorities are trying to adapt existing regulations to cover the unique aspects of NFTs while avoiding stifling innovation in the sector.

Conclusion: Balanced Regulation

Balanced regulation is essential to ensure that the NFT market grows sustainably and securely. While regulatory efforts are underway, the challenge lies in creating a regulatory framework that protects investors and promotes innovation, allowing NFTs to thrive as financial and artistic vehicles in the contemporary digital landscape.

CHAPTER 23:
NFTS AND
ENVIRONMENTAL
SUSTAINABILITY

Environmental considerations have become a central theme in the Non-Fungible Tokens (NFT) industry, especially concerning the impact of blockchain technology on the planet. In this chapter, we will examine environmental concerns related to NFTs and blockchain, and how the sector can evolve sustainably, balancing technological innovation with environmental responsibility.

The Environmental Context

Energy Consumption and Climate Change

The blockchain industry, the foundation of NFTs, has faced criticism for its high energy consumption. Proof-of-Work (PoW) used by some blockchains, such as Ethereum, has been accused of contributing to climate change due to intensive mining activities.

The Technology

behind NFTs

Blockchain and the

Role of Mining

NFTs are based on blockchain technology, which uses mining to confirm and record transactions. The mining process requires a significant amount of electrical computing power, leading to substantial energy consumption, especially in PoW blockchains.

Environmental

Concerns Criticism

and calls for

Change.

Environmental concerns related to NFTs focus on the large carbon footprint generated by token production. This has led to criticism from artists, environmentalists, and communities, calling for sustainable solutions to mitigate the environmental impact of NFTs.

Emerging Solutions

Transition to Proof-of-Stake (PoS)

One emerging solution is the transition from Proof-of-Work to Proof-of-Stake, another consensus mechanism that requires considerably less energy. Ethereum, among the main blockchains used for NFTs, is working on Ethereum 2.0, which will implement PoS.

Sustainable Projects and

Initiatives Blockchain with

an Ecological Focus

Some blockchains are emerging with a specific focus on sustainability. Projects like Tezos and Flow are designed with reduced environmental impact, seeking to offer more eco-friendly alternatives to artists and investors interested in NFTs.

Environmental Offsets and

Green Initiatives Offsetting

Carbon Footprint

Some platforms and artists are implementing environmental offset strategies, committing to offset the carbon footprint generated by the creation and exchange of NFTs. This may include investments in reforestation projects or the use of renewable energy.

Awareness and Education

Informing about NFT Sustainability

Increasing awareness and education about the environmental impact of NFTs is crucial. Artists and platforms can play a crucial role in transparently communicating efforts to reduce environmental impact and raising awareness among users.

Technological Innovations

Exploring Advanced Technological Solutions

The blockchain industry is continuously seeking advanced technological solutions to reduce environmental impact. Some projects are exploring new consensus algorithms, authentication methods, and other innovations to improve sustainability.

Community Engagement

Active Participation in Sustainability

Engaging the community in the transition to more sustainable NFTs is essential. Platforms and artists can work with their user base to implement and support sustainable practices, creating a positive impact through active participation.

Industry Responsibility

Implementing Standards and Improvements

The NFT industry must take responsibility for implementing standards and improvements that reduce the overall environmental impact. This may include adopting more sustainable blockchains, investing in renewable energy, and promoting ecological practices.

Conclusion: A Sustainable Future for NFTs

While NFTs continue to thrive as a form of artistic expression and financial vehicle, environmental sustainability has become a critical priority. Joint efforts between platforms, artists, developers, and the community can shape a future where NFTs coexist harmoniously with the environment, ensuring that digital innovation does not compromise our planet.

CHAPTER 24: THE IMPORTANCE OF THE NFT COMMUNITY

Communities represent the beating heart of Non-Fungible Tokens (NFTs), playing a crucial role in determining the success, value, and longevity of a project. In this chapter, we will explore how community dynamics influence NFTs, creating a vibrant and sustainable ecosystem. We will guide you through the importance of active participation in NFT communities and how it can contribute to your success in the world of NFTs.

The Core of the NFT

Community Creating

an Interconnected

Ecosystem

NFT communities are often defined by a deep connection between creators, collectors, and enthusiasts. These groups form an interconnected core that supports the project, creates a sense of belonging, and fuels enthusiasm around NFTs.

Influencing the Value

of NFTs Community as

the Engine of Value

The strength of a community can directly influences the value of NFTs. A passionate fan base can generate demand, exchange opinions, and promote the project, contributing to its financial and cultural success.

Collectors as the Soul of the

Community Engaging and

Celebrating Collectors

Collectors are often the soul of NFT communities. They create an emotional bond with projects, appreciate the works, and celebrate the artists. Engaging collectors through events, exclusive previews, and personalized interactions can fuel community growth.

Creative Support and

Constructive Feedback

Community as a Source of

Inspiration

NFT communities offer a space where artists can receive constructive feedback and creative support. This ongoing cycle of interaction fuels creativity, pushing artists to evolve and continually improve their work.

Active Participation

Creating a Participatory Environment

Active participation is key to a vibrant NFT community. Creating an environment where all members feel free to share ideas, experiences, and projects contributes to the diversity and vitality of the community.

Community Events

and Initiatives Creating

Engagement and

Enthusiasm

Organizing community events, such as virtual exhibitions, contests, and online meetings, creates engagement and cohesion among members. These initiatives not only strengthen the sense of community but also generate visibility for the project.

Exclusive Access and Privileges

Rewarding Community Engagement

Offering exclusive access and privileges to active community members is a common practice. This can include exclusive previews, discounts, or even the opportunity to participate in key decisions that influence the project.

Growth of Cross-

Project Communities

Interconnection between

Projects

NFT communities often extend beyond the boundaries of a single project. The growth of cross- project communities allows for greater sharing of ideas, collaborations, and the consolidation of a shared culture within the NFT sphere.

Education and Knowledge

Sharing Community as a

Learning Space

NFT communities play an important educational role. Through knowledge sharing, discussions, and shared resources, experienced members can help newcomers better understand the world of NFTs, promoting continuous education.

Collective Problem

Resolution Addressing

Challenges as a

Community

Challenges can arise within the NFT world, from technical issues to controversies. The community can play a crucial role in addressing these problems, proposing solutions and contributing to collective issue management.

Responsibility of Artists

and Platforms Guiding the

Community with Integrity

Artists and platforms have the responsibility to guide the community with integrity. Transparency, open communication, and careful management of expectations are crucial to building a trusting relationship with the community.

Conclusion: Building a Sustainable Future

NFT communities are the foundation on which the long-term success of NFTs is built. Active participation, contributing to growth, and mutual support are key elements in building a sustainable and prosperous future in the NFT ecosystem. The strength of a community can shapes the destiny of NFTs, making them not only a financial opportunity but also a continually evolving form of digital art and culture.

CHAPTER 25: THE PSYCHOLOGY OF NFT INVESTORS

Investments, including those in the world of Non-Fungible Tokens (NFTs), are profoundly influenced by human psychology. In this chapter, we will explore the intricate web of emotions, behaviors, and trends that characterize the psychology of NFT investors. Understanding this dynamic can be essential for those navigating the ever-evolving market of NFTs.

The Frenzy of

Excitement

The Intrigue of

Uniqueness

The unique nature of NFTs, each representing an irreplicable digital asset, evokes a distinct emotion in investors. The prospect of owning an exclusive piece of digital art or a collectible item contributes to the frenzy of excitement, driving investors to participate in this unique world.

FOMO: Fear of Missing Out

The Impulse of "Fear of Missing Out"

The "Fear of Missing Out" (FOMO) is a powerful psychological driver that compels investors to join an investment trend for fear of missing a unique opportunity. In the world of NFTs, where new collections and projects emerge rapidly, FOMO can play a significant role in investment decisions.

The Allure of

Exclusivity The

Desire to Join the

Elite

The psychology of NFT investors is often influenced by the allure of exclusivity. The feeling of belonging to a selected community that owns unique digital assets contributes to a sense of prestige and social status, further motivating investments.

The Community Effect

Sharing Experiences and Advice

The psychology of NFT investors is deeply intertwined with the community effect. Investors tend to share experiences, strategies, and advice within online communities, creating an environment where social dynamics play a crucial role in investment decisions.

The Quest for the

Next Big Deal Hunting

for the Unique

Opportunity

NFT investors are often on the lookout for the next big deal, the next collection or project that could yield significant financial returns. This constant search for a unique opportunity can be fueled by hope and the belief that yesterday's success will repeat.

Information Asymmetry

Impact of Available Information

The psychology of NFT investors is influenced by the

asymmetry of available information. Investors may make decisions based on news, rumors, and information available online, creating a dynamic where the perception of the value of NFTs can vary widely.

Seeking Validation

Investors Seeking Confirmation

The search for validation is a key element in the psychology of NFT investors. Investors may seek confirmations and approvals from the community or prominent figures in the industry to validate their investment decisions.

Loss

Management

Emotional

Impact of Losses

Loss management is a crucial component of the psychology of investors. Losses can have a significant emotional impact on NFT investors, influencing their ability to make rational decisions and manage financial anxiety.

The Tendency

for Overexposure

Portfolio Effect

The psychology of NFT investors can be influenced by the tendency for overexposure. Investors may be tempted to focus on certain collections or assets, increasing the risk of portfolio overexposure.

The Role of

Narrative Creating

a Story Around

NFTs

The psychology of NFT investors is often shaped by the narratives created around specific projects or collections. An engaging story can evoke positive emotions and fuel investor interest, influencing their purchasing decisions.

Conclusion: Navigating the Maze of NFT Investor Psychology

Understanding the psychology of NFT investors is essential for successfully navigating the complex maze of the market. While emotion and enthusiasm play a crucial role, savvy investors can balance these dynamics with a rational assessment of risk and opportunities. Awareness of the psychology of NFT investors can be the key to developing more informed and resilient investment strategies in the ever-dynamic world of NFTs.

CHAPTER 26: ADVANCED RESOURCES FOR NFT INVESTORS

For those looking to delve deeper and enhance their understanding of the Non-Fungible Tokens (NFT) world, it's essential to have access to advanced resources. In this chapter, we will explore a wide range of resources, from online forums to analytical tools, that will enable NFT investors to stay up-to-date and well-informed in the dynamic NFT landscape.

Online Forums and Communities

1.1. Reddit NFT Communities

Reddit hosts various communities dedicated to NFTs. Subreddits like r/NFT, r/CryptoArt, and r/NFTmarket provide in-depth discussions, market analyses, and connections with other NFT enthusiasts.

1.2. Discord NFT Servers

Discord is a hub for numerous NFT communities. Joining specific servers, such as NFT Insider and CryptoPunks, provides direct access to discussions, events, and up-to-date information.

Analytical Platforms

2.1. NonFungible.com

NonFungible.com is an analytical platform that provides detailed data on NFT transactions, collections, and market trends. Investors can use this tool to analyze the historical value of NFTs and predict potential developments.

2.2. CryptoSlam

CryptoSlam focuses on tracking transactions and activities related to NFTs across various blockchains. This tool provides in-depth metrics on the most popular collections and artists.

NFT Markets

3.1. OpenSea

OpenSea is one of the largest NFT markets, offering a wide range of collections. Exploring this market provides insights into new trends and highly sought-after collections.

3.2. Rarible

Rarible is an NFT market that allows users to create and sell their NFTs. Exploring artists' creations on this platform can provide inspiration and insights into emerging trends.

NFT Valuation Tools

4.1. NFT Bank

NFT Bank is a tool that evaluates NFTs based on metrics such as rarity and popularity. This type of tool can be useful for investors looking to identify NFTs with the potential for long-term growth.

4.2. Rarity.Tools

Rarity.Tools provides analyses on the rarity of NFTs, helping investors assess the desirability and growth potential of a collection.

NFT Wallets

5.1. Enjin Wallet

Enjin Wallet is a digital wallet that allows users to manage their NFTs. It offers a comprehensive overview of owned collections and market activities.

5.2. Trust Wallet

Trust Wallet is another NFT wallet that supports various blockchains. It features advanced functionalities for managing and trading NFTs directly from the platform.

Advanced Guides and Courses

6.1. NFT Bible

The NFT Bible is an advanced guide that delves into various aspects of NFTs, from creation to valuation. It is a comprehensive resource for those seeking an in-depth understanding of the industry.

6.2. NFT School

NFT School offers advanced courses on the NFT ecosystem, covering topics such as NFT creation, investment strategy, and portfolio management.

Events and Conferences

7.1. Consensus NFT

Attending conferences like Consensus NFT provides an opportunity to hear from expert speakers, connect with other investors, and stay updated on the latest industry trends.

7.2. NFT Conventions

NFT conventions, such as NFT LA, offer an immersive experience with exhibitions, panel discussions, and direct interactions with artists and collectors.

Social Media and Influencers

8.1. Twitter

Following influencers and key figures in the NFT space on Twitter provides a constant stream of news, analyses, and relevant discussions in the world of NFTs.

8.2. YouTube

Specialized YouTube channels on NFTs, like "The Nifty Show" and "NFT Daily," offer in-depth content, interviews, and reviews of the latest developments.

Conclusion: Expand Knowledge, Refine Strategy

Successfully navigating the world of NFTs requires not only a good basic understanding but also access to advanced resources. Analytical platforms, online forums, NFT valuation tools, and advanced educational resources are all tools that can help investors maintain a comprehensive and informed view of the NFT market. Staying constantly updated with these resources can be key to refining your investment strategy and maximizing success in the dynamic world of NFTs.

CHAPTER 27: FREQUENTLY ASKED QUESTIONS ABOUT NFTS

Non-Fungible Tokens (NFTs) have sparked enormous curiosity and interest, but with the novelty of this emerging technology, many questions naturally arise. In this chapter, we will address the most common questions that investors and enthusiasts have about NFTs, providing clarity on complex concepts and practical aspects of this innovative technology.

What is an NFT?

An NFT, or Non-Fungible Token, is a type of cryptographic token that represents a unique and indivisible digital asset on a blockchain. Unlike fungible cryptocurrencies like Bitcoin or Ethereum, NFTs are unique and cannot be replaced or exchanged at an equivalent value.

How Do NFTs Work?

NFTs operate thanks to blockchain technology, ensuring their immutability and authenticity. Each NFT is associated with a smart contract that determines its properties and usage rules. The blockchain permanently records the ownership and transaction history of each NFT.

What is the Difference Between Fungible and Non-Fungible?

The main difference between fungible and non-fungible

assets is their substitutability. Fungible assets, like traditional cryptocurrencies, are interchangeable at an equivalent value. Non-fungible assets, such as NFTs, are unique and cannot be exchanged one-to-one with other assets equivalently.

How Are NFTs Created?

NFTs are created through a process called "minting." Artists or creators upload their work to an NFT platform and follow instructions to create and publish the token. This process introduces the digital asset to the blockchain, making it an NFT.

What Types of Assets Can Be NFTs?

NFTs can represent a wide range of digital assets, including digital art, videos, music, tweets, games, virtual real estate, and much more. The versatility of NFTs allows artists and creators to tokenize virtually anything.

What Makes NFTs So Unique?

Their uniqueness stems from the combination of blockchain technology and smart contracts. Each NFT has a unique identifier that sets it apart from all others, making it an irreplicable and blockchain- authenticated digital asset.

What Are the Main Blockchains for NFTs?

Ethereum was the first blockchain to support NFTs, but other blockchains like Binance Smart Chain, Polygon, and Tezos are becoming increasingly popular for NFT minting due to lower fees and greater scalability.

How Are NFTs Bought and Sold?

NFTs can be bought and sold through specialized online markets such as OpenSea, Rarible, and Mintable. Buyers place bids or make direct purchases, while sellers set prices or initiate auctions.

What is the Role of Auctions in NFTs?

Auctions are common in the world of NFTs and allow sellers to maximize the value of their work. Buyers can make competitive bids, driving the final price of the NFT to the highest level they are willing to pay.

Do NFTs Have an Environmental Impact?

The environmental impact of NFTs has been debated due to the energy used by blockchains, especially Ethereum, which employs Proof-of-Work. Some blockchains, like Tezos and Flow, use more sustainable alternatives like Proof-of-Stake.

Are NFTs Only for Art Collectors?

No, NFTs are used in various industries, including digital art, gaming, music, and even the tokenization of physical assets. The use of NFTs is continuously expanding, embracing different forms of creativity and industries.

What Are the Main Concerns for Investors?

Investors' main concerns include market volatility, the possibility of fraud, and the management of private keys needed to own and transfer NFTs. Research and caution are crucial to mitigate these risks.

How Are NFTs Protected?

NFT security is essential. Buyers must protect their private keys, use hardware wallets, and conduct thorough research before making purchases. Marketplace platforms must implement advanced security measures.

What Are the Next Developments in the NFT Industry?

Future developments could include the adoption of more sustainable blockchains, the integration of NFTs into the physical world through the tokenization of real assets, and the growth of new sectors like music and film within the NFT ecosystem.

Conclusion: Navigating the World of NFTs with Clarity

NFTs continue to generate interest and questions, and their

rapid evolution makes staying informed crucial. These answers to frequently asked questions provide a solid foundation for anyone looking to explore the world of NFTs more consciously and informedly. With a clear understanding, investors and enthusiasts can confidently navigate the dynamic and stimulating world of Non-Fungible Tokens.

CHAPTER 28: CONCLUSIONS AND FUTURE PERSPECTIVES

The wild race in the world of Non-Fungible Tokens (NFTs) has been more than a passing trend. It has represented a true revolution in how we conceive and interact with digital assets. In this concluding chapter, we will examine the potential of NFTs and the future outlook of this innovative technology, reflecting on how it will continue to shape our digital future and investment possibilities.

The Current State of NFTs

As we conclude this guide, the world of NFTs is still in a state of fervent activity. Artists, creators, investors, and collectors continue to leverage the opportunities offered by NFTs. Markets like OpenSea, Rarible, and others witness a constant fluctuation of unique collections, digital artworks, and other tokenized assets.

The popularity of NFTs has transcended the digital art sector, extending to industries such as gaming, music, tokenization of physical assets, and much more. The blockchain technology underlying NFTs has proven to be a catalyst for the decentralization and democratization of digital ownership.

The Explosive Potential of NFTs

NFTs have demonstrated explosive potential, generating significant profits for some investors and offering artists new ways to monetize their talent. The speed at which they can generate money has drawn the attention of individuals with considerable financial resources, contributing to the growth of the phenomenon of "new rich" in the world of NFTs.

Success stories are not limited to digital art but also extend to sectors like CryptoPunks, blockchain- based games, and tokenizations of real-world assets. NFTs are changing the very nature of digital ownership, opening new opportunities and business models.

Future Perspectives

of NFTs Evolution

of Blockchain

Technology:

Blockchain technology is continuously evolving. While currently, most NFTs are based on blockchains like Ethereum, we will likely see the development of new, more scalable, and sustainable blockchains. This evolution could address environmental concerns related to Proof-of-Work.

Expansion into Different Sectors:

NFTs will extend into unexplored sectors. The tokenization of real-world assets, music, cinema, and other industries will see increased adoption of NFTs. The ability to own and trade digital assets securely and transparently will have a significant impact on various industries.

New Forms of Creativity:

NFTs will stimulate creativity in new and innovative ways. Artists and creators will be inspired to experiment with digital and interactive formats that fully harness the potential of NFTs. This expansion of digital expressions will contribute to redefining the very concept of digital art.

Integration with the Physical World:

The tokenization of physical assets through NFTs will drive the integration of the digital and physical worlds. Ownership of authenticated and traceable physical objects through the blockchain will become a reality, opening new scenarios in the e-commerce and supply chain management sectors.

Technological Innovations:

The evolution of NFTs will be accompanied by technological innovations. More advanced smart contracts, interoperability solutions between blockchains, and new scalability management methods will contribute to creating a more mature and efficient ecosystem.

Regulation:

With the growth of the NFT market, regulatory authorities are likely to increase their attention. Defining clear rules and norms for NFT transactions could contribute to ensuring a safer environment for investors and users.

Conclusion: A Digitally Tokenized Future

In conclusion, NFTs represent an exciting chapter in the history of digital technology. Their ability to transform the nature of ownership and interaction with digital assets is unprecedented. While facing challenges and criticisms, their potential remains undeniable.

The future of NFTs will be written by artists, creators, investors, and innovators who continue to push the boundaries of digital creativity. The integration of blockchain, the tokenization of real- world assets, and diversification into new sectors are just some of the paths that NFTs will traverse in the near future.

We are facing a digitally tokenized future, and NFTs are the key to unlocking the doors of this new world. Whether you are a collector, an investor, or a creative, your journey into the world of NFTs is only beginning. Seize the opportunity, explore innovation, and get ready to witness a future where digital value is a unique, indivisible experience authenticated by NFTs.

EPILOGUE

Concluding this journey through the world of NFTs is like reaching a significant milestone in an extraordinary adventure, but our purpose has always been to prepare you for the digital future. In this epilogue, we reflect on the experience you have just lived and cast a glance at the future prospects of the innovative NFT technology.

A Journey of Knowledge and Opportunities:

We hope that through these pages, you have gained a deep understanding of NFTs, from their technological foundation in blockchain to the multiple applications that are revolutionizing how we conceive ownership, art, and investments. Your journey has been characterized by immersion in fundamental concepts and navigation through the success stories of those who have seen unique opportunities in NFTs.

The Art of Investing and Creating:

We have explored how NFTs are not just a form of investment but also a means to express creativity and create authentic value. Whether you are an investor seeking significant returns or an artist eager to share your vision with the world, NFTs offer fertile ground for the realization of aspirations.

From Present to Future:

Now that you have mastered the complexity of NFTs, it is time to look ahead. The world of NFTs is constantly evolving, and your acquired knowledge positions you favorably to adapt to the challenges and opportunities that the future will bring. Your experience does not stop here; it is only the beginning of a journey of continuous learning and exploration of new digital frontiers.

Responsibility and Sustainability:

The era of NFTs is characterized not only by opportunities but also by responsibilities. Within the digital ecosystem, environmental sustainability is a crucial consideration. By exploring how blockchain technology and NFTs can coexist sustainably, we hope to have contributed to laying the foundations for the responsible use of this innovative technology.

The Power of Community:

We have emphasized the importance of communities in the world of NFTs. Your active participation, knowledge sharing, and engagement with fellow enthusiasts are keys to a rich and fulfilling experience in this digital universe. Continue to be part of this growing and developing community, contributing to its success and enriching your understanding.

The Psychology of Success:

In your journey toward success in NFT investments, psychology plays a crucial role. We have explored how emotions, decisions, and investment trends are influenced by human psychology. Carry this awareness with you on your path, using it as a guide in navigating through market fluctuations.

Advanced Resources and Questions Resolved:

We conclude by offering you further guidance with advanced resources and answers to common questions. Stay informed, deepen your understanding, and remain connected with the community. This will give you an advantage in a rapidly moving world, allowing you to adapt and thrive.

Future Perspectives: The Evolving New Digital:

Finally, the future prospects of NFTs unfold as a territory in constant evolution. Let's explore together the possibilities, imagining a future where NFTs will continue to shape our way of living, investing, and creating. We are only at the beginning of a journey that offers infinite opportunities and fascinating challenges.

We conclude this chapter, but your journey into the world of NFTs is an endless voyage. Whether you are a digital pioneer, a savvy investor, or an enterprising creative, know that the digital future is yours to shape. Lex Digitalis has been your guide, but your story with NFTs continues to be written every passing day. Be bold, be innovative, and keep exploring the vast universe of NFTs.

AFTERWORD

And so, we come to the end of "Lex Digitalis: A Comprehensive Guide to NFTs." This afterword is an invitation to reflect on the immense wealth of knowledge and opportunities you have just explored. Through these pages, we have delved into the depths of the world of NFTs, navigating through complex concepts, success stories, and captivating visions for the digital future.

The Journey as the Destination:

In this journey, you have learned that destiny is not just the attainment of a goal but rather the experience of the journey itself. Your quest for knowledge about NFTs has been an exhilarating ride through rapidly changing digital currents, where each page has been a discovery and each chapter a new adventure.

The Revolutionary Potential of NFTs:

You have gained a profound understanding of blockchain technology and how NFTs are revolutionizing the way we conceive ownership, art, and investments. We have moved from the foundations of blockchain to the peaks of NFTs, exploring their revolutionary potential in various sectors, from art to music, gaming to the tokenization of real assets.

The Symphony of NFTs: Creativity and Investments in Harmony:

NFTs are not just financial instruments; they are an opportunity to express creativity in a new and revolutionary way. We have explored how artists can monetize their talent through crypto art, how collectors can own unique pieces of digital history, and how investors can make foresighted choices in the ever-evolving NFT market.

Responsibility and Sustainability:

You have considered responsibility and sustainability, recognizing that digital progress cannot ignore environmental respect and ethical practices. In the world of NFTs, environmental awareness is crucial, and your understanding of reconciling technology and sustainability puts you in a privileged position to contribute to positive change.

Vibrant Community: The Heart of NFTs:

You have experienced the power of communities, acknowledging that the success of NFTs is intertwined with relationships and connections among enthusiasts, investors, and creatives. Your active participation in these communities is a key to personal growth and collective success in the digital world.

Investor Psychology: Emotions and Decisions:

You have explored investor psychology, discovering how human emotions and decisions influence the NFT market. This awareness will make you more resilient in the face of challenges and wiser in your investment choices.

Advanced Resources: Keep Exploring:

The advanced resources provided are like star maps to explore yet unknown digital territories. Keep searching, learning, and innovating, using these resources as a guide through the challenges and opportunities that the digital future holds.

Your Story with NFTs Continues:

Ultimately, "Lex Digitalis" has been a guide, but your story with NFTs is a narrative still unfolding. The digital realm is a vast and deep ocean, and each day is a new page to be written. Carry with you the knowledge, experiences, and vision gained through these pages as you continue to explore the digital future.

Thank you for being part of this journey. Whether you are a pioneer, an enthusiast, or a digital curious soul, know that your contribution is valuable, and the world of NFTs is richer because of your presence. Be bold, be creative, and continue navigating the digital waves with the awareness that your potential is limitless.

Farewell, digital explorer. Your adventure continues.

ACKNOWLEDGEMENT

In this special chapter of our acknowledgments, we would like to express our deepest gratitude to all of you, dear readers, who have chosen to embark on this journey with us through "Lex Digitalis: A Comprehensive Guide to NFTs." These pages come to life thanks to your commitment and the desire to explore the vast universe of NFTs.

To the Curious and Digital Explorers:

A heartfelt thank you to those who ventured on this path with curious eyes and a desire to learn. Your thirst for knowledge has been the driving force behind every page, and we hope the information contained here has answered your questions and sparked new reflections.

To the Digital Pioneers:

To you, digital pioneers, who have embraced NFTs as a frontier to explore and conquer, our recognition. Your boldness in navigating this uncharted territory is a source of inspiration for all those who follow in your footsteps. May your innovative spirit continue to guide you into even more extraordinary adventures.

To the Creatives and Digital Artists:

A warm applause to digital artists and all those who have embraced NFTs as a canvas to express their creativity. Your works have added color and meaning to this journey, turning the pages into a collective work of art. May your inspiration continue to flow and illuminate the digital world.

To Those Who Shared Success Stories:

To those who have shared success stories through NFTs, our profound appreciation. Your experiences are guiding stars for those seeking to understand the potential of this technology. May your success be just the beginning of a long series of digital triumphs.

To the Insightful Investors:

To you, insightful investors, who have understood the dynamics of the NFT market, we thank you for your trust. Your intelligence and attention are fundamental pillars upon which the success of digital investments relies. May your choices always be illuminated by wisdom and prudence.

To All Enthusiasts and Learners:

Finally, to our passionate and apprentice readers, our sincerest thanks. Your interest and engagement have made the creation of this comprehensive guide possible. May your experiences with NFTs always be enriching and stimulating.

Together, we have created a community of digital explorers, and our thanks are a tribute to your unique contribution to this adventure. May the digital future bring you new discoveries, successes, and a continued sense of wonder.

Heartfelt thanks,

The Team of "Lex Digitalis: A Comprehensive Guide to NFTs"

ABOUT THE AUTHOR

Lex Digitalis

Lex Digitalis is a prominent figure on the international stage, renowned expert, and enlightened thinker in the field of blockchain technology. Born out of an early passion for digital innovation, Lex has dedicated his career to exploring the frontiers of blockchain, bringing the enlightenment of his expertise globally.

Academic Education:

Lex pursued an extraordinary academic career, earning two degrees in disciplines closely related to his passion for technology and innovation. His first degree, obtained with honors, was in Computer Engineering from a technological institute of excellence. This education provided Lex with the solid technical foundations necessary to tackle the complex challenges of the digital world.

Subsequently, Lex earned a second degree in Economics and Finance, thereby strengthening his interdisciplinary understanding of the socio-economic dynamics that shape the blockchain landscape. This unique combination of technical and financial skills gave Lex a holistic perspective, crucial for deciphering the complexities of blockchain and cryptocurrencies.

International Expert:

Lex's career has evolved through roles of international resonance, contributing to projects and initiatives that have redefined how we perceive digital sovereignty. Lex has collaborated with academic institutions, government organizations, and technology sector companies, bringing his wealth of knowledge to diverse contexts.

His constant presence at international conferences, academic articles, and interviews has solidified his reputation as one of the leading experts in the field. Lex Digitalis has become synonymous with innovation and advanced thinking, influencing how professionals, academics, and enthusiasts approach the digital revolution.

Contributions to Technological Literature:

Lex Digitalis's voice has also emerged in technological literature. In addition to curating the "Digital Sovereignty" series, Lex has published seminal articles and essays that have contributed to defining the discourse on blockchain and its global implications. His clear and accessible prose makes complex topics accessible to all, highlighting his commitment to spreading knowledge and fostering a widespread understanding of blockchain.

Visionary and Guardian of Digital Sovereignty:

Beyond his role as an expert, Lex Digitalis is recognized as a visionary and guardian of digital sovereignty. His mission is to promote a responsible and conscious use of emerging technologies, working tirelessly to build a digital future that reflects values of transparency, inclusivity, and decentralization.

BOOKS IN THIS SERIES

Advanced course in digital sovereignty: exploring the future of blockchain technologies

Welcome to the "Digital Sovereignty" Series, a comprehensive and enlightening work that takes you on a journey through the dynamic and ever-evolving world of blockchain technologies. This book series delves into every aspect of digital sovereignty, from NFTs and cryptocurrencies to the fundamental principles of blockchain, providing a comprehensive guide to fully understand its impact and opportunities.

Explore the Digital Future: Each volume in this series provides a clear exposition on key topics such as digital art, decentralized finance, integration with artificial intelligence and IoT, and much more. Each title is designed to guide you through the complex intersections of blockchain technology, providing the knowledge needed to navigate successfully in this rapidly evolving digital landscape.

Advanced Course in Digital Sovereignty: This series is not just a collection of books but an advanced course covering every aspect of digital sovereignty. From the basics of cryptocurrencies and Bitcoin to the tokenization of the real economy, you will explore cutting-edge topics that will define the future of our digital world.

Lead Your Digital Journey: Whether you are a technology

enthusiast, an entrepreneur seeking innovative opportunities, or a student eager for advanced knowledge, the "Digital Sovereignty" Series offers a comprehensive guide. Each book is written in an accessible yet thorough manner, ensuring that anyone can take on the challenge of understanding the complex dynamics of blockchain technology.

Sovereignty and Awareness: Develop a deep understanding of the social, economic, and environmental implications of blockchain. Address emerging challenges, explore new frontiers of innovation, and become part of a global community of individuals embracing digital sovereignty with awareness and wisdom.

One Course, One Vision: "Advanced Course in Digital Sovereignty" is more than just a series of books; it is a path toward a broader vision of the digital future. Prepare to be guided through the world of blockchain technology with authority and clarity, discovering how to shape and understand your role in this new chapter of our digital era.

Blockchain Revolution: A Comprehensive Guide To Emerging Technologies, From Cryptocurrencies To Decentralized Finance And Beyond

Welcome to the ultimate guide to the Blockchain Revolution, an epic work by Lex Digitalis, an expert guide in the ever-evolving territory of Digital Sovereignty. This book represents an essential chapter in the "Digital Sovereignty" series, a collection of enlightening texts that delve into the depths of blockchain technologies, guiding readers through a complex and fascinating journey.

Explore the World of Cryptocurrencies

In this volume, Lex Digitalis unveils the secrets and potential of blockchain, from the evolution of cryptocurrencies to the revolution of decentralized finance (DeFi). Through accessible yet profound language, the reader will be immersed in a detailed analysis of the concept of value throughout human history, exploring the roots of strong and weak money and shedding light on schools of thought related to monetary policy strategies.

Bitcoin and Beyond: Lex Digitalis goes further, revealing the advent of Bitcoin, with an in-depth look at the innovations that this cryptocurrency has brought to the financial world. With narrative skill, the mystery of Satoshi Nakamoto, the enigmatic inventor of Bitcoin, is explored and speculated upon, while the main operating modes of the cryptocurrency are unveiled.

The Digital Sovereignty Series: This book is not just a standalone work; it is a milestone in Lex Digitalis' "Digital Sovereignty" series. Each title in this series is designed to offer a comprehensive guide on key topics such as NFTs, cryptocurrencies, decentralized finance, governance, regulations, and much more. Each text is an open window to the digital future, guiding readers through the intricacies of a world increasingly driven by blockchain technology.

Who is This Book For: Whether you are a technology enthusiast, an entrepreneur seeking innovative opportunities, or a knowledge-thirsty student, "Blockchain Revolution" is the compass that will guide you through the complex and fascinating waters of digital sovereignty. Lex Digitalis offers a unique perspective, transforming complex concepts into an accessible and stimulating educational journey.

Become a Digital Explorer: In conclusion, this book is an invitation to become digital explorers, to push beyond the boundaries of the known, and to embrace the blockchain revolution with awareness and wisdom. Lex Digitalis leads us through a journey of discovery, providing not only knowledge but also an opportunity to shape our role in the digital transformation.

Prepare for an unforgettable journey into the heart of the Blockchain Revolution with Lex Digitalis as your enlightening guide.

www.ingramcontent.com/pod-product-compliance
Lightning Source LLC
LaVergne TN
LVHW051335050326
832903LV00031B/3552